# POTTERY: FORM AND EXPRESSION

## BY MARGUERITE WILDENHAIN

### PHOTO STORY BY OTTO HAGEL

AMERICAN CRAFTS COUNCIL
PACIFIC BOOKS, PUBLISHERS / PALO ALTO, CALIFORNIA

The photographs that were taken for this book were meant as a tribute to the skill and craftsmanship of the potter — that and nothing more. Pots and potters are indeed of this earth, and any other connotations belong in the realm of the human imagination. Reality is the measure of life; concepts of truth can be tested in the give and take of conflicting opinions.

OTTO HAGEL

Photographs for the jacket, the frontispiece, and for plates 1 to 63, 71, 86, 94 to 97 are by OTTO HAGEL

First edition published 1959 by the American Craftsmen's Council.
Enlarged edition published 1962 by Reinhold Book Corporation.
Reissued 1973 by Pacific Books, Publishers.

International Standard Book Number 0-87015-202-5.
Library of Congress Catalog Card Number 62-16374.
Printed and bound in the United States of America.

PACIFIC BOOKS, PUBLISHERS
P. O. Box 558
Palo Alto, California 94302

Few people have been given the privilege of influencing their students to the same extent as Marguerite Wildenhain. Born in France of German and English parents; educated and teaching at the Bauhaus in its first exciting phase of freedom and renewal of creative conceptions; coming to the United States in 1940 and settling in California as a producing potter; ultimately opening her own school at Pond Farm; lecturing and conducting seminars in many educational institutions of the United States. Such has been her background and from this rich tapestry of life she has evolved the philosophy of work and the relation of the individual to his work and creative activities so vividly expressed in this book.

It is not a "how-to-do-it" book. Reading it the potter will not be a better technician but he will have a deeper understanding of himself, his purpose in work and his relation to the creative act. In this respect it will be good reading not just for potters but for all craftsmen. Mrs. Wildenhain's personality, her enthusiasms, her convictions, cross the usual barriers offered by print and paper and she seems to be sitting in the room with the reader, talking in her own words, stimulating thought and discussion.

The American Craftsmen's Council is happy to have had some share in making it possible to bring this book to Mrs. Wildenhain's many friends. They in turn have, by their advance orders, assured its publication. This is a happy pattern of procedure which the Council hopes to be able to repeat from time to time.

Aileen O. Webb,
Chairman of the Board
American Craftsmen's Council

I wish to express my thanks to those who have helped me in the production of this book: in the first place to Otto Hagel for his unending patience in taking the photographs that I needed, for his great understanding of my problems, for the skill with which he interpreted my ideas in his medium and for the many excellent suggestions he gave me.

To Dr. Paul Friedlander, Yolanda Newby and Lucretia Nelson I owe gratitude for their painstaking reading of my manuscript and for valuable advice; I must also thank the British Museum, the Victoria and Albert Museum in London, the Fitzwilliam Museum in Cambridge, England and the Musée de l'Homme in Paris for giving me the right to reproduce several of their fine pieces of pottery.

To many of my fellow-potters I am grateful for their willingness to lend me photographs of their work and to my students as a whole for having been the very much alive objects of my studies.

M.W.
Pond Farm
Guerneville, Calif.

To my Masters Max Krehan and Gerhard Marcks
in gratitude.

# CONTENTS

*"It is not a soul, 't is not
a body that we are training up, but a man
and we ought not to divide him."*
*Montaigne*

# INTRODUCTION

This is more than a technical book. I shall touch technical points only insofar as I think that they are important in the education and the development of a young craftsman into a complete man. To escape the danger of generalization and empty abstraction I have used technical examples of the depth of basic knowledge and of the intensity of human effort that are required if we want to educate craftsmen to be more than one-sided technicians.

The aim of this book is to make clear that it is not enough to teach techniques. We want to develop young people for a wholesome and hopeful generation,–—— for a generation which believes in the value of the humanities, which will face the problems of our time honestly and without fear, with the deep will to understand other men and to learn to build a better future.

Technique alone, without any moral and ethical point of departure or aim, has brought us to the very edge of a universal catastrophe that we have in no way overcome. To achieve this necessary future victory over ourselves and the terrifying world that we have created, we will need to find again a synthesis between technical knowledge and spiritual content. It is not a question of the crafts only, the problem is as wide as the whole of human civilization. Unsolved, it will be fatal to all mankind. It is thus for everyone of us––craftsman, artist, teacher, scholar or scientist––to help build towards a more human way of life, one that can lead man in the coming generations to personal dignity, integrity and peace.

But generations are made of many single individuals, each with his special abilities. We can either develop these to maturity or we can let them go to waste. We can lead a student towards a sound, human and creatively intelligent point of view or we can corrupt him totally. If we want the life of man as a whole to have a deeper content, with a cultural basis, we must educate every single human being to find a deeper spiritual content for his own life. Neither peace of mind nor "happiness" can be bought by machine, money, success or a high standard of living. Man must make the effort himself and develop his way of life from the very depth of his own being. The real revolutions, truth and lies, originate in the minds of men. There it is that we must start to clarify, to educate, to build up.

The technical problems of education are necessarily different in the various fields, but human problems are basically the same for all fields of the mind. We must develop, cultivate, inspire and discipline the creative and spiritual abilities of man. We must not waste, corrupt or slant for material purposes those qualities that make him more than an animal: his sense of beauty, his idea of truth, his ability to think, his creative intuition and his vision of God.

We know that there are many men and women——artists, scholars, teachers, scientists——lost in the wide world, in big cities or the backwoods, in schools and colleges, in factories and on farms, people deeply disturbed by the current materialistic trend, people who are searching for more than they are finding. It is essential to give them affirmation and hope, to coordinate all their efforts into a more conscious group of honest workers towards an aim that has human dignity and personal integrity.

Craftsmen of all times have battled with the materials they have used, with the difficulties of the technique, with the problems of form and expression. While in the more primitive times the main difficulties lay in the technique, in our times of technical advancement the real problems lie almost wholly in form and expression. We have solved many technical difficulties and most of the restrictions of materials and machines; but we have lost in the process of an increasingly materialistic education, the essential relation to nature, to man and to God.

Those problems that loom so large before us cannot be solved from the top down, in vague general lines, in conferences and educational meetings. We will have to start at the very basis of human occupation and of thought. As one of the oldest basic occupations of man, pottery, I feel, may well be chosen as a representative example for similar issues in parallel fields.

What are the problems in teaching the crafts in our times? Why is it apparently so difficult to develop creative craftsmen who are able to convey their own ideas with excellent craftsmanship, honest conviction and complete integrity?

10

How is it that with all our perfected techniques we have failed to rear those craftsmen in our generation?

To be a craftsman apparently requires a definite attitude towards work and life, something evidently few schools are able to convey, something that cannot easily be taught in courses on techniques and theories. Mass school education quite naturally consists of more or less abstract and impersonal ideas, facts and techniques. To a large percentage of students all this is being conveyed en masse and with a conformity that is apt to restrict the thinking process and the personal struggle of a student towards maturity. Instead they impose certain rules and theories that will bring him quick results and a degree. This will limit the scope of his feelings, of his thoughts, his ideas, his likes and dislikes, his personal conception of art and his total growth as a man and as an artist. There is something that a young student must learn, something formative and essential that he cannot easily get in our school system. It is something that he gets in the daily contact with a man who has worked and has concentrated all his energies in that one special field he has chosen as his life-work. The daily interchange of ideas, of experience, of thought, the common interest of student and teacher in the solving of the recurring difficulties of their profession——not in a classroom but in an actual life situation——will necessarily bring the student close to the way of life of that master. An intuitive understanding of that man, his attitude, his standards, will help the student to a certain assimilation of all that the master represents and this assimilation becomes obviously a part of his education and his personal development. This is the all-important issue.

Thus, if I manage to convey something of this essence, of this spirit to the reader in the following pages, so that the subject matter becomes for him a creative experience, I shall have achieved what I somehow foolhardily set out to do.

*M.W.*
*November 1958*
*Pond Farm Pottery*
*Guerneville, Calif.*

# Chapter I / THE POTTER IN OUR TIME

The fact that this theme was chosen as a first chapter seems to indicate that there must be some question, and some doubts, as to the relation of the potter to our time.  Has the world really changed so much that a craft, which has been a human occupation ever since man has been man, has become obsolete in our times?   Has life bypassed the potter as those four-lane highways bypass picturesque and quaint little villages to which one looks back with envious sympathy, but in which one would not want to live any more?  Has pottery still some essential meaning for the human race, or is it only a relic from former times like the hoop skirt and the bustle?  Let us examine our problem closely.

Man has needed and still needs pottery, vessels to eat and drink from, to store liquids and solids in, for experiments in the technical fields, to wash and bathe in.  He needs insulators, bricks and tiles; and these, we take for granted, will in our progressive time, of course, be made by the contemporary industrial set-up.  We never question the urgent necessity of these mass production centers.

But we do question the value of the work of those individual men and women who make their pots by hand without taking what we call "advantage of the machine" to go in for a larger production; because they seem to be old-fashioned, full of atavism in their outdated standards of quality, of workmanship, of integrity and pride in their work; because for them work seems to be more than a question of supply and demand and time.  Instead it seems for them to be a natural fourth dimension of all things that are good and beautiful.  In short, we may question the value of those people because they do not seem to fit into our pattern of living any more.

To find out whether these hand potters still have a right to live and to be taken as valuable citizens of our world, I should like to examine the process of making pottery by hand and see what human activities are involved in the process.

*A potter in our time:*
*no machine can achieve the variety.*

But I must start at the very beginning and at the origin of things, at the relationships of form and thought, of matter and idea, of man and thing, of man and God.

Creative work is made of two different and well-separated activities: one all spiritual, I would say––the idea; one all concrete––the making. Our problem will be to trace those two parts to the point of their total fusion in an object and see whether the activities involved and the characteristic development of the craftsman are of importance to the human race or not.

At the beginning of all man-created things is the idea. Eidos in Greek was something that you reached with your eyes, through your sight, by the process of seeing; it was that which is visual and seen. The form that you saw with your inner eye was "the idea." Plato says: "The inner eye is more important to keep than ten thousand real eyes, for only through this can truth be seen. The soul has an eye to see and it is directed toward the eternal forms."

Most of us have eyes of the soul that are weak and incapable of seeing what is God-like. The creative man is the one who sees the "eternal forms."

With an "idea" in front of his whole being, with his form-idea in his mind, the artist starts to work with his hands. For him each time it is like the first day of creation; there is nothing but a blank, a chaos, a darkness of desire and urge; and he must plunge into that part that is most true in him, into that source where pure imagination comes from, where all learning is forgotten and does not count any more, where he is at the source of all things and totally alone.

For art is not cumulative and progressive as is science, and no artist can begin where his predecessor left off, but must start like primitive man, so to say, at the origin of things.

So here is the artist, in our case the potter, working. With the first movement of his hands in touching the clay, thousands of problems creep up like so many temptations to lure him away from his pure, original idea. He is trying to force or to coax his very concrete medium, that formless clay, into the form-idea that he has before his inner eye.

14

This strange interplay in the artist between the pre-existing idea and the work itself causes the craftsman constantly to split himself so as to create: that "idea," that form that he has in his mind dominates every movement he makes, and thus the growing object stands under the continuous pressure and the sceptical vigilance of his inner vision. But matter has laws as much as truth has, so the potter tries to learn them; he finds out, or is lucky to be taught, those methods that are apt to favor better results; he will learn those movements, those rules and restrictions that will bring his work to more certain success, and he will find out that it is to his definite advantage to know and to respect them.

After much laboring effort and many disappointments, he will have acquired what we call "the technique." But that should not mean an exacting formula, or a set pattern, or too narrow and strict conditions. Those would have the bad effect of allowing the potter to dispense with thinking and with deciding in a thousand delicate matters of responsibility to form. For the field is unlimited for the craftsman with an open mind; he will look for new materials to suit his new needs, invent and develop new methods, and those may require new tools. These again will allow him functions that he could not have solved with his hands only. As a result a whole new set of possibilities and techniques will evolve.

So the craftsman not only chooses his tools but becomes himself the tool of his idea; he brings together what he wants and plans with what he can do and knows, what he can see and touch. He chooses and organizes size, methods, materials, techniques, for that one chosen circumstance. He orders diversity toward one aim, and out of chaos grows form.

For this complex procedure, certain human qualities are imperative; for perfection, even to the most talented, does not come easily. To realize a perfect fusion between the vision from the inner source and the excellence of execution we will need complete consecration of a man's existence and all available forces and abilities of the total man.

This daily struggle with his work, this closing himself up with his innermost self in a laboring toil of concentration and coordination, the challenge of the difficulties with materials and methods—all this cannot help but develop in the craftsman qualities of endurance, self-discipline, patience, healthy self-criticism and the ability of focusing his total capacity on one great aim.

For the artist-potter is like the priest: he has dedicated his life to something that is greater than he——to beauty, expression, art. And, strangely enough, the potter has to achieve this spiritual feat physically, with his hands, and working in a tough and unsophisticated material. Clearly, somewhere there must be a more than usual synthesis of heart, mind and hand. And this is the fact that, for me, will always give value to hand pottery, if it is creatively alive, in any age, and especially in one as mechanically-minded as ours.

Today, as I see it, we have lost that intimate correlation of the mind and the hands as a philosophy of life, as it was in the centuries when crafts were all-important; we do not feel any longer the real possibilities of those wonderful tools, our hands, "that can give and receive, tear and heal, bless and beg, curse, tie or smite, be hammer, nipper or spade," (Valery) according to what our minds choose them to be. We do not use our hands creatively any longer, in more than a technical sense; not in a way that conveys an ethical, poetical and, I should even like to say, religious point of view.

So, if we look at the pots of the last few generations as a whole, we cannot help but find most of them wanting, because they do not convey what makes a pot really good: a sound technique, an imaginative and functional form and a personal idea.

How have we come to that state of affairs? Don't we have all the technical knowledge, all the machinery and expensive experimental equipment, all the materials, costly or common, finely-ground or coarse as we choose? Haven't we several thousand years of good pottery in our ancestral background, and more than that, even; also the knowledge of the excellent work of all cultures of the world: Chinese, Indian, Incan and others to look at and to learn from? And yet, compared to theirs, are our pots not lacking in skill, in expression and in beauty? Why? T.S. Eliot says: "Good prose cannot be written by people without convictions." And, I should like to add, nor good pots made, either. And, as we are today, we have no convictions, no real faith in ourselves, in our work, or in our values; we have no ethical philosophy of life that allows us to set a free pace of our own. We have not the conviction to choose our ways of living, any more than we choose our words, our thoughts, our standards of art, religion, beauty. We trust blindly

16

in the propaganda values of this or that way of life that is advertised; we are afraid of our own personal feelings, of poverty and unpopularity, of lack of success, of being either old-fashioned or highbrow in our points of view; we believe in practical half-truths in daily use but we do not see that these are also half-lies.

We have lost a deep relation with nature and, with that, our natural instinct which is part of our best, our divine substance and much purer than all reasoning. We have both corrupted our instinctive feelings and neglected them so we cannot trust them any longer. And so we have lost "that powerful simplicity of purpose" (Conrad) of life and work, of mind and hand united in one creation of man.

Our difficulties thus lie, apparently, in the field of ethics and human values and not in the technique.

In order that hand pottery shall survive and be valid again, so that it shall become a virile, unsentimental and creative activity, it seems to me urgent to raise anew the standards of the crafts, above the sentimentality of the dilettante and the dead traditional standards of former centuries; and also above intellectual tightrope walking and materialistic opportunism, thus fearlessly giving the craftsman a true and more complete relationship between his work and his life.

For to know a specific craft really and deeply, as I mean it, brings to a man more than a salary and some success; it enlarges and edifies his whole being, it builds up his ethics and his esthetics; without his being aware of it, perhaps, it brings him in touch with everything that is essential in life so that he may in the end rise to the understanding power of a philosopher.

So, we must work with constant devotion——lose ourselves in what is greater than we are, in order to find ourselves. And we will mature, and some element will become visible in our work that comes from our innermost experience in life, something that no techniques, nor any amount of historical training or courses in "design" could ever foster, something that is our own, and unique. For if a thing is conceived in the depths of our being, we will find a way to express it; it may be crude and unskillful, but it will be honest and intelligible.

This will also explain why it is not possible for us to go back to the forms of times that are passed, to the standards of beauty of other countries——those of Greece or China or the 18th century or others, be they ever so excellent. We are not these people any more; we live, think, love differently, believe in other values, move on other planes, and have a greatly accelerated pace. So other forms, not theirs, will become necessary for us, just as we wear other clothes, have other houses and travel in other vehicles than they did.

There is nothing frightening nor unhealthy about this. Creative men have always made things according to their own ideas without looking too much to their predecessors; our old catherads show it repeatedly, as each generation has added to the whole in its specific way. Plants, too, change their forms within a genus according to urgency and environment; they grow larger or smaller leaves, hairs and spines as needed. So must we adapt ourselves. We are living now in what is the most arid and desolate time for art, and in order to survive we shall have to find those basic forms again that are alone the essential growing cells of creative work and life. Only then will handwork survive and only then has it the right to survive.

As a potter, I visualize the way to come close to that ideal in the following way: It is mainly a matter of the education of those young people who want to become craftsmen. Put them first through a thorough training at the wheel or in other handwork with an excellent teacher. Those who are not able or willing to go wholeheartedly into it will drop out soon; the others should not be spared any instruction in processes, materials, techniques, however tedious or difficult. But above all, whet their desire to learn, fire their initiative, their urge to understand not only the things that are visible, but also those that are closed up in the heart and mind. "The chief thing is to have a soul that loves the truth and harbors it where it finds it." (Goethe)

This training will be arduous and somewhat rough and toilsome, but not without deep compensations, and out of blind impulse there will grow vigor, ardor and work-discipline, and——if it is there——talent, too. Teach the students to use materials according to their innate possibilities, with understanding, restraint and feeling; open their eyes to form, to line, to color, to proportion. Interest them in tools and functional problems. But above all, teach them to discern honest expression from fake glamour, original feeling from borrowed emotion, genuine form from that which is simply traditional or fashionable.

Let them abhor the blind imitation of whatever is in fashion or brings success (as for example, Sung or Bauhaus) and rather let them be awkward and humble than smart and dishonest. For it is not just techniques that we are teaching or a job and success that we are promising; we are trying to develop creative and honest craftsmen in our time.

First and foremost, let us give to the younger generation all that we still have of a living tradition, not only the technical knowledge, but the way of life integrated with those traditions, For that is the essential element to quicken the heart of the young person who wants to work and live in a creative profession. And let us also take from the machine, from new tools and materials, all the ideas and suggestions of form, methods, training that these make possible. We cannot ignore them and remain really alive. Let us admire the pottery of former ages and countries not blindly but seeingly, and let us learn to discern what qualities make the beautiful serenity of some Greek pots and what qualities infuse with fierce untamed beauty those from Peru or Africa.

Let us study the lives of those men and women who lived for an idea, whether artist, saint or scientist——accepted by society or not! Let us take time to learn, to watch, to read, to understand, to develop, to think. Let us look into nature and the supernatural; let us look at, admire and be awed by the unending ingenious diversity of all forms of nature: rocks, seed pods and leaves and flowers, shells and feathers; from the smooth silky bark of a madrone tree to the sharp hardness of a leaf of holly; from talc to lava and from sponge to coral——a whole natural scale of textures, of surface and form expression, of ingenious devices to solve functional problems. Let us watch with open mind and eyes the birds build their nests, the bees their hives, and see in the forms of the ants how function decides form.

Let us look at man. Let us travel to other lands and see other peoples, other art, other customs, other forms of living and thinking. It will make us more conscious and also more critical of our own, and we shall have to decide afresh where we are going. Let us learn from the so-called "primitives" the magic relation of art and religion, and from our own past, our cathedrals for instance, a Christian counterpart of both.

And let us take the education of the talented young people, who want to become craftsmen, out of the classroom atmosphere of schools and into the invigorating winds of life. It will be easier to help them develop into honest, excellent artisans who know their craft as an engineer knows his mechanics, thoroughly and efficiently; and who have above all a deep personal and artistic integrity. For the "new craftsman" of tomorrow will have to learn to see his trade again as a whole, as something that requires his total personality, his ingenuity, his skill, his reflection and his faith——only then will there be a basic cultural quality to his work and to his life.

No single craftsman, however, be he ever so excellent, can possibly turn the tide of standards. But in a group with other groups I can see the attitude towards work changing considerably in a few generations. So, let us unite internationally all those men and women of good will, of imagination and talent, who are or want to become craftsmen. Let us form small productive workshops, in groups of creative teams, where each one works to the best of his abilities as a creative artisan. As a group with many other groups in all fields of the crafts, it is readily imaginable that they could in time not only influence the quality of industrial production, but, what I feel to be much more important, develop a sounder way of life for themselves and for the public in general.

The "new craftsman" must be trained to use with dexterity and understanding all hand methods and those of mass production too. He must be able to use them with discernment, efficiency, expedition and without emotional conflict, just as we can walk, or drive a car without making an emotional problem out of it. He may be the ideal designer for industry as well as an excellent creative artisan individually. He will be able to use the machine to his advantage, but he will not adore it, nor will he blindly copy or adore that which has been made by hand and handed down by tradition. In this way he will bring to his own personal work, or to industry, standards of workmanship and quality. His designs will be genuine and honest, for he will have taken root in a creative activity that has a cultural basis. If he has to repeat his work, he will try to do it not like the machine——blindly——but always better and in unending variety, with changes and modulations. Thus he will, himself, develop with his work and in his work.

To sum up, I would like to say that I do not doubt the necessity of keeping potters and other craftsmen in the picture of our "new world."

More than that: not only must crafts as such remain an occupation of man in the future, but, as I see it, they are one of the roots from which a more hopeful civilization can grow. When more men and women are willing to live with one basic idea in mind: the unity of work and life based on an ethical conviction, then we shall have a chance for a valid human civilization.

In an age when the "Universal Declaration of Human Rights" is proclaimed for the first time as the highest aspiration, not of one nation only, but for all the people of the world, it seems to me that the artist and the artisan are perhaps those who stand the nearest to that ideal; for, throughout his whole life, the artist will have chosen as the measure of all things, not money, nor success, nor power nor the machine, but man, the very genuine essence of man.

# Chapter 2 / THE CLAY

The material of the potter is a dangerous and elusive substance——the only one, I think, that can be used without any tools, as it comes from the ground. Most common, though most complex, it has a wider range of uses and greater potentialities than any other natural substance. It has no definite form in itself. It is the ground on which we tread and it is the bottom of the oceans, but it can be pressed, coiled, pinched, thrown on the wheel, cast or jiggered into any form imaginable. It can be made to look smooth as butter or gritty as coarse gravel; it can be polished to a glossy sheen, or remain dull and earthy. It can be liquid, viscose, malleable, plastic, or hard as rock; it can be translucent and delicately fragile, or be refractory and withstand extreme pressure and heat. One can fire it at a low temperature with camel-dung or buffalo-chips on the open field; or pass it through the highest degrees of heat in complicated gas, oil or electrical furnaces.

One can cover it with slips and glazes in all colors of the rainbow; one can paint on it, on or under the glaze with different materials——metal oxides or clays. One can use brush, slip-tracer or wax-resist; one can scratch, cut drill, engrave, polish and sandblast it. It can be made to look like almost any other material that exists, but in spite of all those nearly unlimited metamorphoses, there are only a certain number of forms and expressions that are truly characteristic of our material, clay.

To find just these forms, that is, to find a synthesis of material and form, of material and expression will be an important part of the work of a potter; for ultimately that most common material will have become either beautiful or ugly, costly or vulgar, expressive or insipid, according to whatever the potter has chosen to do with it.

Since, as we know, the clay is of no value in itself, it is evident that the values found in the end-product will depend entirely on the idea and the skill

*Plate No. 1/ The clay has no definite form of itself; it is the potter's aim to give it form.*

of the potter on how well he was able to use his medium to its full expression—— that is, on how thoroughly he mastered the techniques as well as how clearly the form and the whole character of the pot was conceived in the mind of the craftsman.

It will thus be imperative to know, first of all, what you want to make, not to allow the clay to force itself on you, but rather to force the clay into whatever form you are planning. Different forms (tile or cup) will require different clays; varied methods (cast or thrown) also will require a variety of materials. From the beginning, it will have to be a choice, a limitation, out of an infinite variety of clays, until you find the one that is best suited not only to fulfill all technical requirements but also to convey your conception, as a potter, in relation to beauty, tactile expression and form-idea.

There is something very satisfying, stimulating and conducive to creative experiment in the fact that the clay itself has no value: it is not gold, so no one will be afraid of smashing a pot, if he has not succeeded; but will go on trying again and again.

Though the clay has no form of its own (Pl. 1), it is still as essential a part of the total design of a piece of pottery as the form, the glaze, or the decoration: it is the very stuff of the pot and will necessarily have to be chosen by the potter with sensitive understanding and discrimination. To one potter, a smooth light-colored clay might greatly appeal, while to another a dark, rough, grainy clay might open up most creative ideas. A third, again, might be at a total loss with all but translucent and vitreous porcelain. It is evident then that we should not merely copy or take over other potters' clays; it is their own choice of materials and may not be at all suggestive to you of all the possibilities that lie in the clay.

Thus, for the student-potter one of the basic experiences will be to become acquainted with the clays, and that he will have to do with his own hands. No one can do that for him, and one cannot over-emphasize the importance of the intimate relation of the hand to the clay. (Pl. 2)

To learn the possibilities that lie unborn in the clay, it will be essential to work with it in every imaginable way: to play with it, pinch it, roll and scratch

24

Plate No. 2/ The potter gets acquainted with the clay through his hands and chooses the one that suits his needs and ideas.

it, to wet, roughen or smooth it; to make it look light and silky, or deeply textured or sculptured, dark and roughly carved; to try to get out of it every single mood and character that lies in it——and all this, preferably, with just your fingers. There are innumerable possibilities, and to discover those will be an unending, exciting and creative experiment. There is no limit to ingenious inventiveness. No two people ever make the same patterns. (Pl. 3) Up to sixty different textures have been made by one student, with his fingers alone, without even touching on the limits of the potential results: from deepest relief of "dinosaur tracks," to the finest, most delicate silky surface treatment; from the primitive and simple impression of just one finger, to the most complex motions of pressing, pulling, lifting and twisting of all the fingers simultaneously.

To understand the plasticity of the clay and what that means as an element in pottery, it is essential that one also learn to treat the material three-dimensionally. It is advisable to take a slab of clay and bend or cut it in as many different planes as possible, or add slabs to each other in free form, or in relief. Those exercises will open up to the student ideas that he may never have thought of; they will develop his sculptural sense and will make him conceive his pots in the round——an ability that is not easily developed and is too often overlooked.

The student will also have to discover what happens to his clays in the firing process; he will have to figure into the conception of his pots not only the plastic quality of the clay, but also the color, the change of expression that occurs when the material is transformed from the malleable to the fired state, and when it has shrunk to its final size.

This finding of one's own special material, I mean just the right one to convey one's individual ideas most easily and most adequately, is a struggle that cannot be resolved through courses in design, nor by tradition, nor by lectures: it will have to evolve from the potter's own artistic sensitivity and creative imagination.

*Plate No. 3/ A finger explores some*
*of the possibilities in treating his material;*
*a thousand other ways are possible, too.*

*Plate No. 4/ Forms of nature:*
*quartz crystals on a piece of black lava.*
*Every material has its specific form.*

28

# Chapter 3 / EDUCATION TO FORM

To make pottery means, as we have seen, to give form to a material that offers many tempting possibilities. Not for nothing is man said to have been made out of clay, it is the basic stuff of life——and, just as a poet who might want to write about mankind, after a year's experience of life, would fail, so the potter who thought he was a competent potter after the same length of time would obviously fail, also. It takes years to find valid and genuine forms and it takes all the skill, intelligence, feeling, experience, talent, discrimination and integrity of a man. It is in the widest sense a problem of human development and of how to pour the sum of a man's experience of life into form.

What then is form?

A crystal in the mother rock (Pl. 4) or a seed pod of a plant (Pl. 5), also an engine and a razor blade (Pl. 6), but also a Marcks' sculpture (Pl. 7), a sonnet by Shakespeare and an aria from Mozart.

Forms of nature grow independently from man as the result of natural circumstances: a seed pod cannot be made by man.

Forms of technique and forms of art exist only because man can think, feel, invent and because he has hands; they do not grow, they are made. They require certain human qualities, intelligent reasoning, conceptual thought and the talent for transmuting an idea or an emotion into a form.

In the technical form the origin of the problem lies in the use for which the form is meant, in the materials, the physical forces and the mechanical procedure, but the emotion of the inventor is not necessarily a part of the end result. (Pl. 6)

In the forms of art, on the other hand, the need for giving form is first and ulti-

*Plate No. 5/ Seed pod of a bottle-brush tree; nature finds a form for each need.*

mately a human experience of the man creating it. "Never forget the first impression that has touched you." (Rodin) A sonnet or a piece of sculpture is the external image of an inner vision that existed only in the mind of its creator. There is thus an initial emotion, a perception of a form, a medium to express it, but not necessarily any outside aim or use. (Pl. 7) The form of art is in itself complete, perfect and unique. Forms of technique and forms of art overlap in many cases, in all the crafts, in architecture for instance, where the creative impulse and the laws of materials, techniques and function have to be fused in a living object. (Pl. 8)

We shall thus try to formulate more specifically our problem in pottery, in the following way: it is to create forms out of a formless and boundless multitude of clay masses, forms that have originated in the conception of the potter, that have grown out of his idea of beauty, his skill as a craftsman and his total intelligence, feeling and belief as a human being.

Those forms must convey to the spectator, through their lines and volumes, and an expressive tension that comes from within, the emotions and ideas that urged the potter to make those special forms.

For not just any form, but expressive form, imaginative and live form is the aim of a potter. To arrive at that you will need more than a certain amount of technique and traditional skill. It is evident, though, that you will have to struggle first with the plain hard matter of technique and master the pulling up on the wheel of a cleanly thrown pot or the simpler methods of coils and slabs. That the throwing on the wheel in itself is a skill requiring more than average patience, energy and physical coordination, the potters all know. If you conquer

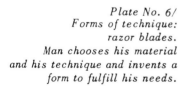

*Plate No. 6/*
*Forms of technique:*
*razor blades.*
*Man chooses his material*
*and his technique and invents a*
*form to fulfill his needs.*

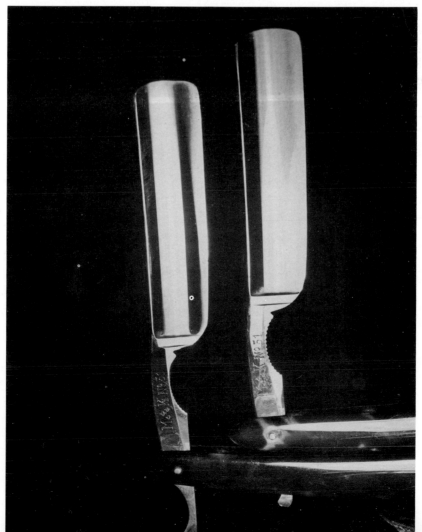

*Plate No. 7/ Form of art: a sculpture by Gerhard Marcks.
An artist has vision and creates
a form to convey his emotion and idea.*

32

*Plate No. 8/ Form of craft:*
*a jug. It should show the*
*synthesis of a*
*form of technique and of art.*

the wheel, that technique is of immeasurable help in speeding up the process of production; but if you do not learn to control the centrifugal force and to use its momentum to your advantage, the wheel will be the most frustrating and inimical device you can imagine. To all struggling with it, the wheel will at first seem to be clearly an invention of the devil. (Pl. 9 to 24)

But once you know how to throw, you have wings.

*Plate No. 9/ An inert lump of clay is patted onto the wheel; the wheel is at rest.*

*A SERIES SHOWING THE PROCESS OF THROWING A POT ON THE WHEEL*

Plate No. 10/ The wheel spins; the lump of clay is centered in a double movement;
the fingers pull horizontally towards the center while the thumbs press vertically down.

*Plate No. 11/ The fingers of the left hand gently open the centered lump of clay; the right hand helps for steadiness and pressure.*

Plate No. 12/ *The hands widen the base opening as required. The left hand
presses horizontally across to the right, while the right hand presses vertically
down moving to the right at the same speed as the clay is pushed out with the left
hand. The hands are interlocked for more coordinated pressure and steadiness.*

37

*Plate No. 13/ In a claw-like movement, both hands*
*pull towards the center and upwards: the clay starts to rise.*

Plate No. 14/ *The left hand is inside and presses the clay out, the right knuckle follows the bulge and presses inwards; the double movement makes the clay climb.*

Plate No. 15/ *The movement is repeated till the lump of clay has been pulled as thin as possible with the use of fingers alone; a tall cylinder stands.*

40

*Plate No. 16/ A strong pressure from outside*
*will keep the top of a pitcher from widening out of control.*

41

*Plate No. 17/ Both hands meet at the very top;*
*a gentle pressure between the fingers will keep the rim cleanly horizontal.*

*Plate No. 18/ Another inch or two in height and a more precise thinness
of the cylinder can be reached if one uses a rib. Again the left hand, inside, presses out,
while the right hand follows with the rib and presses inwards.
The double movement gives to the cylinder its ultimate thinness.*

Plate No. 19/ A tall hollow cylinder stands but it has no definite
form as yet. The left hand uses a rigid inside tool,
the right hand a flexible outside one. Here, too, it is the left hand
that pushes outwards while the right hand regulates and corrects.

44

*Plate No. 20/ The movement is repeated till
the belly of the pitcher has the wanted outline.*

*Plate No. 21/ The belly is completed and*
*the neck is now narrowed from the outside.*

Plate No. 22/ Another half inch in height can be pulled out of the now still narrower neck; a wet sponge and the fingers will do the trick.

*Plate No. 23/ The pitcher is thrown and*
*will now be cut off with a twisted copper wire.*

48

*Plate No. 24/ The pitcher is lifted off the wheel;
the whole procedure has not taken ten minutes.*

When you know how to throw well, quickly and deftly all the plates, bowls, pitchers, cups and saucers that you have been taught to make; when you can produce decent teapots with spouts that pour and lids that fit, then is the time to try more consciously for personal forms, for more imaginative pots, for wider experimenting along the whole line of your creative abilities. Then is the time for developing those forms that you would make if you had never seen a pot before, those that are your conception of what a pot should look like.

But at this point, I would like to warn most earnestly not to try to find your "own expression" before you are capable of using your medium and your technique perfectly. It also does in no way mean ignoring all that men have done before you and starting out as a blank page. No one could do without that which we have all inherited from former generations, all that is an intrinsic and inseparable part of all of us, nor would there be any advantage in dropping that inheritance, even if it were possible. All the past generations, the extinct cultures, all have formed us in a certain way, have influenced each of us uniquely, according to our ancestors, country, inherited talents, limitations, education and stage of development.

Patience is all-important; you will have to train not only the hand, the eye of a student, his sense of touch and his artistic skill; you must also open up his mind to line, to volume, to color, to problems of tension and balance; but above all you must teach him to discern between real living form and sentimental or dilettante form substitutes. This process is naturally slow, it requires an intense opening up to everything that is important in life: to nature (Pl. 25, 26), to man, to science and to religion. It is in the truest sense a matter of teaching the student to find himself and to develop his utmost possibilities.

It might seem to the reader that much of what I have mentioned above has little to do with pottery directly. Not so, though: this curiosity to learn things that have nothing in common with your own field of interest, this sharing with others in other fields of human occupation, just this understanding of their problems, their aims, their ways of thought and of work is of great importance to a craftsman: it will save him from becoming a pedant, a specialist, a man who knows only about one thing in life, who is not interested in other occupations of man and who thus can have only an extremely narrow outlook on life.

50

Plate No. 25/
A child looks at
nature and draws;
it is never too early
to start looking.

Plate No. 26/
Adults too have to
learn to see: a student tries
to separate the essential
forms from the accidental ones.

51

*Plate No. 27/ From a multitude of forms of nature
the student chooses a few for study.*

It is only when a man can broaden out from the center towards a more comprehensive picture of mankind, that he himself grows as a man. When he can include, at least to a certain extent, the other arts, philosophy and religion in his picture of the world, he can hope to become an artist and not remain a technician. Every piece of knowledge, of vitally experienced learning, every deeper contact with other fields of activity will open up some hidden corner in the man who is learning. He will grow and as he grows he will want and need more and deeper knowledge. At the end of his life perhaps that which he has learned will have become assimilated; and his own and "personal form" will have quite naturally evolved as the result of his development and of his own wisdom.

To elaborate on this opening-up process of a student, let me give just one example from an unlimited number of possible and similar ones.

As a potter working with clay, he will be interested in looking over the hills for possible clay deposits and will soon find that a certain amount of knowledge of geology would help him locate these. The laws of mountain formation and erosion will help him to understand the composition and the formation of clay deposits; he will learn why some are clean (when they lie where they have disintegrated from the original feldspar) and why some are dirtied with all sorts of materials that they have carried with them on the long path from their site of origin to where they lie now. The time element involved in these processes will awe him beyond expectation if he is not an absolute blasé. And as he goes over those deposits he will learn why some are fat and others are meager, why some are white and others red or blue or yellow. Also he will find soon that only certain plants seem to grow on those clay hills, while others don't. If the student is at all inquisitive, he will wonder why and will start looking into the vegetation around him; he will become interested in botany, in soil and rock composition, and that will bring him, from another side, into his chemistry. Also, as he gets interested in plants, he will of course study their growth from the seed pods and watch the development and the variety of forms during that process. Or, while studying geology he will find rocks and crystals and be struck by the diversity of the forms that inorganic nature invents in order to succeed in her lawful development. (Pl. 27) The most modern of artists cannot imagine more abstract shapes than crystals have, nor more fantastic forms than the seed pods of the most common weeds. Then, as he looks at the ingenious functional devices and structural stratagems that nature has figured out to solve whatever problems faced her, the student will get a very interesting object lesson in the functionalism of forms, in tectonic engineering. He will discover that every living object, plant, rock, man and beast has a precise and specific form (Pl. 28), that every surface has a different texture, every texture its own reason and a different expression. He will find out that natural forms are made of an unending variety of elements, apparently distinct from each other and still intimately related to each other and to the whole. It will probably dawn upon him that the same is true of forms of pottery, and this closer acquaintance with nature will give him inspiration and thrill.

And, if he has a meditative mind, he will also look at man and his occupation in the district where clay lies; he will see that the potters have always settled as near to their material as they could, especially in former times when transportation was a problem. He may also discover that the clay that they found and used has been responsible for certain techniques and practices that became the characteristic elements in the production of that part of the country. He will thus discover the potteries from Kentucky and Tennessee, the stoneware potters from the Rhine or the Faenza pottery from Italy and others. As he looks into the work of those men in their natural habitats, there is no end to the things that he will get involved and interested in: the ways those men lived and worked, what they thought and believed; how all this influenced the pots they made and what these looked like; what the techniques and the themes of their decorations were; what their religion and their art were. He will also see that there never is anything stagnant in life, how all forms varied through the ages as inventions, ideas and techniques moved through the lands, and how one country learned from another.

So the whole world is open for him to discover, for his investigation, for his research and for his education. He can learn from all nations and all times, from good and bad. No human expression is without value for whoever wants to learn, whoever aspires to a more complete vision, whoever is honestly inquisitive and wants to improve his total judgment.

Life is not a mechanical and technical process, so it is evident that abstract information and techniques cannot be an end in themselves of the education of man. All this knowledge must not remain something in the brain only, a bare accumulation of data and names, a cold registration of facts; those would be of no use as such to a creative man. No, everything that a man learns should change him in his innermost self, should clear his mind more and more of false assumptions, of a hodgepodge of unclear concepts and ideas; it should make him expand and long and search for truth over ever larger and deeper areas, areas that he formerly ignored and could never have imagined.

It is a known fact that the more one learns, the more remains to be learned and the more it seems that one will never reach that total view one is aspiring to. But, is that not the best of life? One never reaches an end (one only: death);

54

but as one tries and searches his capacities seem to multiply and to grow. That all this cannot be arrived at consciously is evident, you cannot go out and be sure "to grow wise." I can only say that there is some chance of getting to the real depths of things, of thought, of art and truth, if you are open for learning and for the search towards the things of the mind——and none if you do not seek for that wisdom.

When work and life have a really deep relation, when the former is, so to say, the manifestation of what a man thinks, feels, lives for, knows; when the spiritual content transcends the material knowledge, real form will then grow silently as the natural result of a man struggling with his materials, his techniques, his emotions, his ideas and his knowledge. Those forms then will have some of the growing qualities of the forms of nature, something that has surpassed the technical form and is alive. For, whether it is a Sung vase or a pot from Peru, a statue of a devil or of God, it is what man puts into his work of intangible values that ultimately decides form.

But, as in nature, where the sum of elements of different forms and functions (heart, lungs, blood, etc.) makes the total live man, so in the realm of form there are different fundamental constituents that are essential for the life of the whole, elements that are only held together by the spirit and the idea of a man. Form also requires a certain alphabet that, to a certain extent, has to be learned. There is a relation of volumes and planes to each other, but that is not enough. Since apparently the inner vision of the creative man expresses itself through the medium of those parts, those volumes, those different elements, it will be to our definite advantage to learn something about these.

*Plate No. 28/*
*The student tries*
*to convey with the simplest means*
*the form elements,*
*the proportions and the character*
*of what he is looking at.*

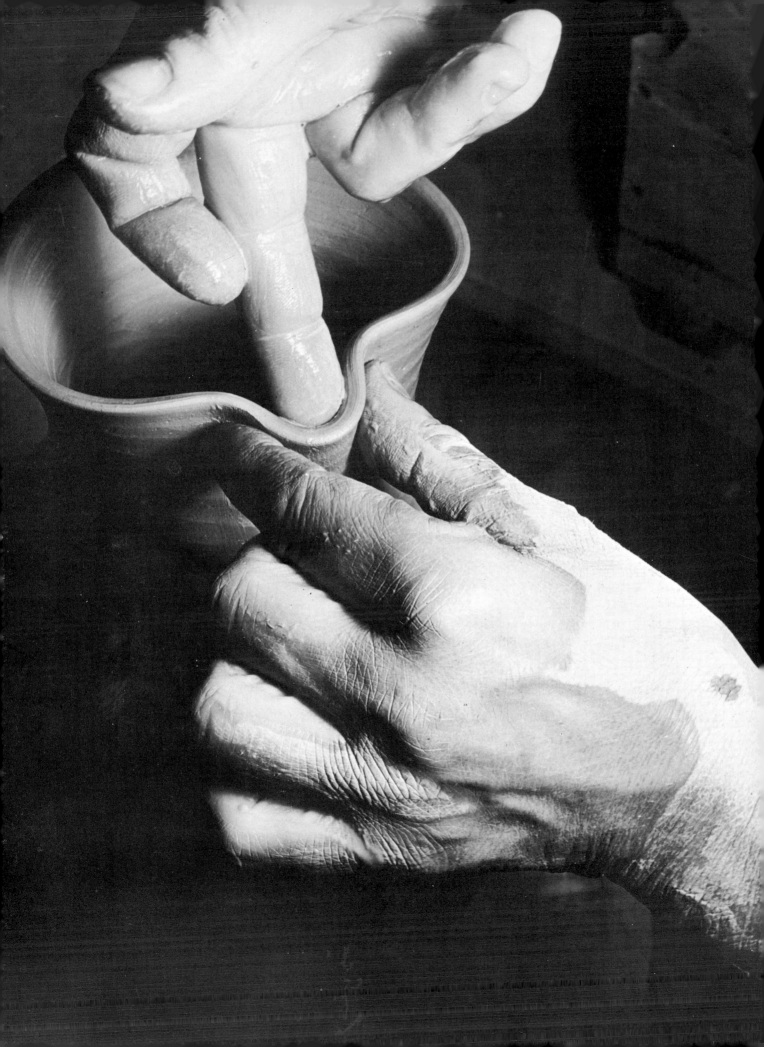

# Chapter 4 THE HAND AND THE FORM

Up to recent times, ever since pots were made by hand or on the wheel, all forms invented by the potters were closely related to their hands. Rims, bellies, spouts, necks showed distinctly that the hand of the potter had been decisive in figuring out those forms. A spout of a pitcher had that specific form, that unabstract, live form because it was actually discovered through fingers, and not abstractly, as a theoretical concept in the brain, but through the contact of a finger with its material. (Pl. 29) If a spout had been carved with a knife or had been pressed into a mold, its basic shape would have been completely different.

Not only in the details was the hand responsible and creative, but all forms reflected more or less the bodily character of the maker: a healthy potter with strong hands made a sturdy rim and powerful bellies on his pots. One with more delicate hands and smaller proportions made his spouts and rims narrower, the feet of his pots more delicate, the bellies more sensitive. One with more than average dexterity of the hands made elaborate, extravagant forms, perhaps more stilted feet, more subtly differentiated lids and spouts. And simple souls with simple movements and hands made, all in all, simple pots. (Pl. 30)

More than in any other craft, there is thus in pottery a direct and primary relation between the hands and the form, an intimate contact that cannot be eliminated without taking away a most essential quality from the end product. An imaginative pot copied by an ever-so-skilled worker can be only like a duplicate, a copy, a second-best.

Nobody can force the understanding between the hand and the form, but one can develop the sensitivity of the hands to a great extent. It takes time and effort; the will to learn the technique is not enough. It is also necessary to explore tactile experience to the utmost limit of its possibilities. To find

*Plate No. 29/ Feeling the possibilities*
*of the material, the fingers invent*
*the form of a spout.*

new ways of treating materials, of developing forms that are not mere, traditional hand-me-downs or copies from other cultures or other potters, it is essential for the potter to experiment with his material, with form, tools, techniques. He must learn to use his hands as the marvelous tools they are meant to be, to let those fingers be form-giving by consciously speculating, discovering, accentuating with them those forms that are possible; by letting them lead him wherever they want without fear of making bad pots, by warming up in the process of throwing to an alertness that requires his complete attention and devotion, by rising to a sensory susceptibility and a sensitivity that can read the visual phenomena as they occur under his hands in relation to the total picture of the object that he is making.

Clumsy, ungainly, unbalanced and unsatisfying pots will naturally be the result at first, but let us not be afraid of these; let us see that they are so and learn through our errors and failures to discard them as exercises for later, better pots. Outside the boundaries of the forms and techniques handed down by tradition, there are unlimited others, unborn as yet; the imaginative potter discovers them and makes them his own.

This experimental relation of the hand to the form is not essential only during the beginning period; it is in no sense merely a trial period that one must quickly get through. On the contrary, it is a very fundamental part of the whole potting process. The more the potter is able to carry into his maturity his initial alert sensitivity of the hand to the form, the better potter he is. For it is necessary for the creative potter to burst the limits of tradition and the restrictions of convention and to shatter the limitation of his own routine.

Plate No. 30/ Fingertips are the brain and heart of the potter;
forms are invented right there. A rim takes form.

# Chapter 5 / THE MATERIAL AND THE FORM

All materials have intrinsic and characteristic form elements; to discover these and to be able to use them not only technically to their advantage but also as part of the sum total of the form-expression of a piece of pottery is well worth a potter's study.

Here, as always through the whole process of apprenticeship, it is a matter of opening the senses and the mind to exploratory work in a special field, of making the young potter alive and awake to the different characters and expressions that various materials will take on and of being capable of feeling their relationship, their similarities and their differences. It is not only a matter of technique, of knowing that certain clays are smooth, others coarse or gritty; it is somehow a much more intuitive sense, a feeling in one's mind and fingers that will make it, in the end, "natural" for us to use the right materials for whatever technique we choose. We come back, of course, to the basic relation of the hand to the form mentioned above.

To work with a material that is formed either in the liquid or malleable state and that hardens to rock through a process of firing will necessarily require a thorough knowledge of the stages of its transformation. But it is still more important to realize the fact that, depending on the basic composition of the clay, different forms are possible and suitable, and to use this fact with understanding. (Pl. 31, 32) A meager tile or terra cotta clay with either fine quartz or coarse grog will lend itself to quite another range of forms than would, at the other end of the scale in ceramic materials, a high-fired vitreous porcelain body. Thus a teacup or a pitcher made out of stoneware clay by a potter with a conscious feeling for his material will differ widely from those that same potter would make in a fine translucent porcelain; in their whole character and in every detail they would differ—in the thinness of the main body, in the distribution of the separate volumes, in the curves and angles of spouts, feet, bellies and handles; and they would besides ask for a totally different range of decorative treatments. (Pl. 33, 34)

There is thus a danger in having students make a "design" for some object if they have no thorough knowledge of and relation to their material. Such designs will only touch the problem superficially and impersonally, because no good design can be detached from its material which is the substance of the object. Everything that is alive and original in the designer's mind must pass, as it were, through the screen of the material before form and material can be fused in a good piece of craft. There is another misconception that is common in our times: the idea that anybody can make a "design" for anything if he has some taste and perhaps some "art training." It is just this lack of closeness to the materials that is the case of many poor designs in our contemporary production, as is obvious to the initiated.

Thus, if we want to make good pots, we will first find it necessary to fuse two elements: form and material. Let me quote from Paul Valéry: "The indissolubility of the two elements (form and material) is the aim of all great art. It is through this search for a connection that has to be felt and accomplished inside of the vibrating depth of the artist and in some way in his whole body, that his works will acquire some resemblance to the living products of nature in which it is impossible to dissociate the forces and the forms....Our great builders have always clearly conceived their work in a single burst and not in two movements of the mind or in two series of operations, some related to form and some to the material. If you will allow me that expression: they thought in their material."

To think in his material is the potter's aim. It will allow him to put into clay that which he visualizes in his mind without either forcing his material to some expression that it cannot have, or coercing his own images into the concrete restriction of some alien material.

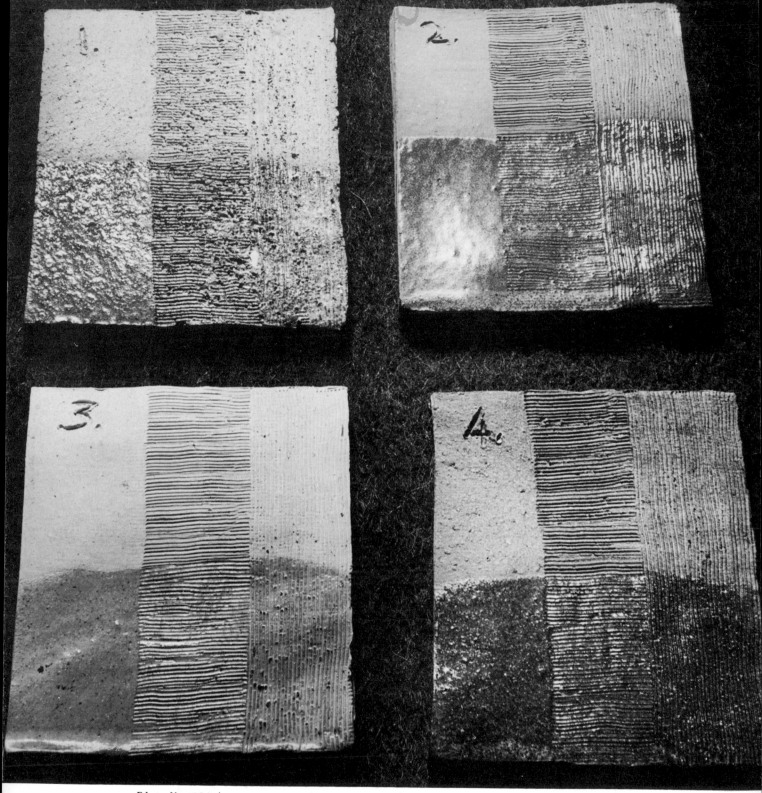

*Plate No. 31/ A coarse groggy clay (1), a slightly grainy reddish clay (2),*
*a very smooth white clay (3), and a dark slightly gritty clay (4)*
*are all treated in the same way. Their differences in character were not sufficiently*
*taken into account and so the results are not characteristic for the materials.*

*Plate No. 32/ The groggy clay (1) is highly textured; a thin glaze barely covers the reddish clay that is used as an intermediate color between white and brown slip (2); a thick glossy opaque white glaze covers the smooth white clay (3), while dark lines accentuate the whiteness of the main parts; the unglazed black clay (4) is used in contrast to a light glazed background. To accentuate its grainy character the unglazed parts have been textured. The four clays have been treated according to their innate characteristics.*

63

*Plate No. 33/ The stoneware cup is simple, clear and straightforward.*

*Plate No. 34/ The highly translucent porcelain cup is sophisticated and elegant, more subtle and delicate than the stoneware cup in its form.*

# Chapter 6 / THE FUNCTION AND THE FORM

All pots are functional, even those that are supposed to be purely decorative, for that is their function.

To solve the problem of use and function in reasonable relation to the material is the next step to a good piece of pottery. Since we all want to make decent cups and saucers, handles that fit the hand, lids that do not fall off or slide around, spouts that pour and do not drip, we find that usefulness and functionalism are important subjects of thought for a potter. These problems, however, can be solved with a normal amount of intelligence and do not require any special human emotion or wisdom. They require from the potter only perseverance and a somewhat mechanical turn of mind, plus the will not to be satisfied till he has found the best possible solution for whatever was his functional problem.

If he has a teacher to show him how to make spouts, lids and handles, it will be to his advantage, for men before him have faced the same problems and have found many ways of solving them basically. This is where tradition is all important; it will save him years of dabbling around.

But function also has its definite fineness—something that is more than the rough solving of a technical process. It is not enough for a spout to pour; it must pour in the right amount, not like a watering can in a coarse jet two inches in diameter, that floods the cup and the carpet; it must also pour at the right angle, as you would naturally pour into the teacup without having to make a special effort to have them meet: the poured-out tea and the cup. (Pl. 35) The spout, moreover, should start at some special part of the belly—usually rather low for a teapot, since you do not want the tea leaves that float on the top of the water to clog the sieve inside the spout. And the spout should be long enough not to spill if you should tilt the pot slightly while carrying it or before pouring.

A lid on a teapot and one on a cookie jar must be different despite the similarity of their functions. (Pl. 36) The covered jar (Pl. 37) needs a cover large enough to let the cookie out and also the hand with the cookie; while you will want to give the teapot the tightest and smallest possible lid to keep the fragrance of the tea from escaping. This lid should rest securely on the top of the teapot and not fall out when the pot is tilted to pour. (Pl. 35)

That form is closely related to function must be obvious by now; but the fine differences in the treatment of functional problems need more than the ability to solve functional problems in general. Something is needed that transcends technique and function and that carries over into the realm of form. Let us suppose that we have thrown a good-looking cylindrical coffeepot for which we now need a lid. The ordinary, slightly convex lid fitting with an edge overhanging the width of the pot would make an already rather wide pot look still wider; it would seem top-heavy and would, in fact, be so. You would have to hold the lid in place every time you wanted to pour. But, if you throw a slight rim inside of that same cylinder, about three-quarters of an inch below the top of your pot, onto which you can sink your lid, that lid will become smaller in size and lighter in weight. Also it can be tilted without falling out and will make the whole coffeepot look more delicate and refined. By sinking the lid and changing its form, from its original convex to either a concave or horizontal form, you will modify still more the whole character of the lid and so of the pot. The knob also plays a definite part in the function of a lid and must be made to fit the fingers without slipping; it can perfect or spoil a lid and thereby the whole pot: whether it should be high or low, round or free form, hollow or solid, will depend on the rest of the pot and on what you have in mind. (Pl. 37)

This is just one example of the importance of one detail; but pots are made of many details, each of which has equally unlimited possibilities; handles, spouts and lids are the test pieces for the ingenuity, initiative, the skill of a potter. Different objects will require different solutions and those again will develop into more delicate and diversified forms. Throughout the years the potter will build up a whole store of efficient and beautiful solutions to functional problems, for good functional solutions have a definite, clear beauty and should not be hidden away. To think of making a lid look like the con-

*Plate No. 36/ The tea caddy has a double lid and the smallest possible opening to prevent the fragrance of the tea from escaping.*

*Plate No. 35/ The teapot pours easily, the lid does not fall out as the pot is tilted, the handle is easy on the hand.*

*Plate No. 37/ The knob of the lid fits the fingers, the opening of the jar is large enough to let the hand pass easily.*

Plate No. 39/ The potter's wheel:
the age-old kickwheel
is still more adaptable,
more sensitive and responsive
than the best electric wheel.

irregular form, impossible to throw on the wheel, or an accuracy and precise-
ness that former methods could not have. They also had a more complex and
composite constructional character. (Pl. 42, 43) Since the pot was put together
from several parts that had been pressed separately, there was scarcely a limit
to the diversity of the forms that were possible, or to the number and the variety of the parts that could, in the end, be put together, in the leather-hard state,
to form a unit. That complexity, that structural composition, that certain hard,
clean-cut look was again their character and their beauty. (Pl. 44)

Pots cast in plaster molds in our time allow again for a wider range of forms,
forms of quite different expression from those pressed into molds. If the latter
showed a structural character, those cast from liquid clay show, to the extreme,
that liquid and plastic quality of the loose poured clay; they seem to have
grown rather than to have been constructed. In fact, they seem just barely to

71

*Plate No. 38/ Coiling*
*has a beauty of its own:*
*the technique creates*
*the patterns of decoration.*

have solidified from the original formless mass under the magic spell of some artificer who knew how. The nearly unlimited possibilities of that method are, of course, tempting to all sorts of bad taste; but let us overlook the fact that, with good taste and understanding, cast pieces have their definite beauty, too.

Let us, then, look upon the technique as one of the parts essential to the whole, like the hand, the material, the function; let us understand how to use our methods according to their main and particular qualities. For any pot has to be thought (that means felt and conceived) with respect to the technique, too. To want to make a square pot on the rotating wheel is obviously a paradox; just as paradoxical, though for the beginner perhaps not quite as obviously so, is to try to make a machine-made pot look handmade. It is a mistake to

*Plate No. 40/ Pots thrown on the wheel have a blown-out-from-the-center expression and a clear total form.*

think that a pot will have a "richer, handmade look" if it is pressed into a mold and then retouched or decorated a bit. It most probably will be a fake: neither an honest, pressed or cast piece nor a fully handmade, personally expressive pot. In trying to hide the method and cover up its qualities, one has slanted its basic character and it will have lost its characteristic expression. Anything that one does to it on the surface will only accentuate that which one wants to hide.

That firing techniques have to be taken into account as an essential part of the form-idea is self-evident. The transformation of the material itself, its shrinking to a smaller size, the change of color and texture of the whole character of the clay is so important that it cannot be stressed enough; you have to be intimately acquainted with the whole procedure before you can make a pot that is really your own. Certain forms cannot hold their weight as they soften in the fire, certain angles will collapse, certain cuts into the basic and self-sustaining circle will twist or crack in the firing—all this is part of the technique that we must know.

As we have seen, no single technique is either good or bad if it is intelligently and well used; so let us be honest about our methods too: each one of these has its own, very characteristic beauty, and it is up to the potter to discover these and to form his pots accordingly.

At this point, I should like to digress a moment and touch on a problem that seems to cause many a headache to many a young craftsman: the relation of the craftsman to industry and to the machine.

An increased population and demand, a higher standard of living and with that, the need for more and more diversified objects, have forced man into an industrial setup that we cannot ignore. No reasonable potter, though, will fight this situation with the fear that he may "lose his soul as an artist" if he works in an industrial setup. On the contrary, I have found that cooperation with industry is a very challenging and excitingly interesting affair and should like to advise every student to work in a pottery factory for a substantial period. One cannot help learning much from the technical research, the efficient methods, from the thoroughness with which problems are thought

74

Plate No. 42/ The stoneware
creamer is thrown on the wheel
and the handle pulled
from soft clay right on the
creamer; a certain sturdiness
and simplicity are the
obvious result and expression.

Plate No. 43/ Though basically
the same shape, the jiggered
porcelain creamer shows a more
composite character:
the spout and the handle have
been pressed separately
and added later; the form
is thus more complex.
Royal Berlin Porcelain Manufacture;
design: Marguerite Wildenhain

75

through to the end; and also one cannot help admiring what the industrial set-up could make possible, namely, to produce good pots by the millions and at prices available to everybody.

I have said before, and want to stress again, that there will always be need for the craftsman and the individual worker, not because of their production (which is small, anyway) but because of the human development of the man himself; still I do want to remark, on the other hand, that there is nothing anomalous in a well-trained potter's making models for mass production. (Pl. 34, 43, 44, 45) It is a much cleaner solution than to try to repeat by hand an unlimited number of identical pieces; that can only result in killing any original talent, imagination—and, in the end, the whole man—in the process. No, let us consciously use the machine and the industrial setup whenever we have to go into greater production. A potter who knows his craft has an unlimited store of forms in his mind and in his hands, forms that have evolved out of the long years of training, of intimate contact with the material and all its problems. His forms cannot help having more life, more warmth in their lines and volumes, more real relation to the material, the technique, the function, the process of fabrication than all those drawn on paper by "drawing-board designers" who have hardly ever—or perhaps never—worked in clay.

So, let us use the machine when we need it, but let us not adore it. It is a necessary tool, no more. To have machines and to know how to use them efficiently does not mean that we are participating in a higher civilization or in a way of life that makes for better, more enlightened and wiser men. To use the machine creatively is possible, however; this should be the artist's aim. If we agree that the means of production cannot be the aim of a man's life, it will not be difficult to see what place the machine should hold in his life. The craftsman will not, then, have to be afraid of "losing his soul" if he works for a factory and makes models for mass production. And it certainly will require that he face squarely the very special problems involved in the process of mass production, the time element necessary for the making, the cost of fabrication, the machines or methods used in the reproduction process. None of these factors need touch his artistic integrity or lower his standards of quality; but he will have to acknowledge them as actual technical problems and will have to solve them as best he can, just

Plate No. 44/ A factory-made porcelain tureen shows a more constructional character and does not hide the process by which it was made: the forms remain separate and clear as they were pressed. Royal Berlin Porcelain Manufacture; design: Marguerite Wildenhain

as he deals with all the other problems he is accustomed to solve in his daily work.

But let us come back to the technique. I can hear from some of my readers: "Yes, that is just what I want to know: what about glazes, bodies and firing techniques; where are the recipes?"

I have made it clear in the introduction that I did not plan to write a technical book; of these there are many excellent ones, much better and more complete than I could ever write. I did not feel that there was any need to add another one to an already confusing array, nor that I should be the one to write such a book if it had been necessary.

Quite the contrary—I felt that one thing had to be stressed in our times and in our country, namely, that the knowledge of techniques is not all that is required if one wants to make excellent pots.

Let it be said clearly, however, that of course it is imperative first for all of us to have a certain amount of technical knowledge at our disposition. I mean that there must not be ignorance of those things a potter has to know: the fundamental throwing on the wheel, the basic understanding of bodies and glazes, the experience with kilns and the process of firing, etc. It is obvious that years are necessary to acquire not only the bare rudiments of the techniques but also wholly to master them, and that those difficult techniques cannot be learned from books alone. But it may not be quite as obvious to many of our potters that these techniques also have, so to say, to sink into the very flesh and blood of the potter, that they have to disappear as "techniques," that they must fade from consciousness and be totally forgotten in the process of working.

Let us not hold up the technique as an end in itself. The "how-to-make-it" is only the very first beginning; it is like learning the letters of the alphabet, no more. "Stoneware," "salt glaze," "reduction," "wax-resist," "Japanese brush stroke" and so on are no more than shop talk, and mean absolutely nothing as to the quality of a piece of pottery. Within the

range of all techniques there is ample scope for the best and for the worst.

Techniques were invented by men; they did not fall to the potters like manna from heaven. They are not God-given, eternal and divine. They are, rather, very frail and human and vary and disappear with the different races, over the years and the centuries. They are like the growing pains of mankind in the strenuous process of trying to form materials according to a diversity of needs and ideas. If different men in different times invented different techniques it was because those special techniques were the best they could invent for what they needed and for what they wanted to express. What we need and what we want to say should form our techniques, just as the thoughts and needs of former generations made them invent, each in due time and place, their own various techniques. What is essential above all is to have something to say, something that is valid enough to be said in our own terms and for which the inherited techniques may not be fitting nor adequate.

Technique alone has no depth of meaning: as in poetry, where the most perfect technique in rhyme and verse, without a valuable thought and emotion behind it, would not make a poem of any significance, so too with pottery. Technique is but a way to make something. Whether that "something" is of human value will depend on what the potter has to say and how he uses the technique to convey that idea to others. So, here again, as through the whole education of a craftsman, it becomes more important to develop the potter as a man than as a technician, so that, as he grows and his ideas clarify and mature, he will be able to invent and use his own techniques.

Let me explain further: for the man with small talent and little imagination, technique will be all-important, because that is all he will ever be able to reach; he will learn techniques and will use them just as he has learned them. He may even become extremely skillful in usage, so that the innocent spectator might be impressed and awed by his technical skill. But it will not fool the more understanding critic who will see that there is nothing behind that skill, that this "know-how" does not convey any idea beyond itself; that it is creatively sterile and thus has little human value. The strange fact is that here "technique" has destroyed the man. In the process of his development,

80

the man was not strong enough to assimilate and absorb the technique; so the technique has absorbed him—there is nothing left of human heart and head. Technique has vanquished the man.

On the other hand, a talented man with imagination and force will not basically need the technique to convey what he feels and thinks. (Remember the beautifully innocent and technically unskilled paintings of Rousseau and see how he used the medium according to his very special needs and feelings.) The creative man will invent his own ways and his own techniques, and, if his vision is clear, he will convey what he means to the outside world without hesitation or confusion.

It is evident that neither of these cases is ideal. But if I had to choose between the work of a skillful nonentity and that of an awkwardly-expressed creative personality, there is no doubt that I would choose the latter.

Let it be clear, though that this "awkwardly-expressed personality" will always remain an insufficiency, a shortcoming, an imperfection. For the more talented a man is, the finer and deeper the thoughts and emotions he wants to express, the nearer he gets to the eternal truths, the more difficult it will be for him to convey these to mankind; and the more will he need to master techniques so as to be able to convey his ideas to the world.

Thus it is clear that the creative and talented man needs the technique, too; but that will grow with him under the regulating and vigilant power and the control of a higher intelligence and vision. The technique in itself will not get an ascendency over the man, but rather will it be very much subjected to the ideas and the conceptions of that man. In this case "technique" will not have destroyed "man;" on the contrary it will have made it possible for him to express in an expert and excellent way all he had been able to feel, to think and to imagine.

# Chapter 8 / THE DECORATION AND THE FORM

There are innumerable ways of decorating pots, either with a glaze of more or less brilliant color, or with some design; but like a lovely dress over an ugly or deformed body, the most beautiful glaze or the most elegant design over a badly-shaped pot will only show the discrepancy all the more.

So you should use glaze and design not to make pots that are insipid "look like something," but because you want to express or accentuate that which was in your mind when you conceived and made that special pot. Those pots that have been clearly conceived in the form are the easiest to decorate; the volumes of that form will force you to certain lines at certain spots, or to certain divisions of the main body. If you can read the sculptural alphabet of a pot, at least you can decorate in a basically sound way but, of course, there can be more to decorating a pot than that; there is no top limit to art.

First of all, do not try to decorate a pot for which you had no idea to start with. Intuition is the first necessity. Not all pots need be decorated if they have good forms. And, if they have not, it will not save them, either.

Do not make a design on paper, except as a shorthand note for something that you might forget otherwise. The design must be conceived in the round; pots are all three-dimensional and the design must fit them like a skin. Thus, no design can be figured out in detail in advance of the pot; the pot is the architecture and the primary element. Every line that you make will have to accentuate that which the volumes have already expressed in the form. Lines are powerful, and a line at the wrong spot will destroy the best pot, while a single line at just the right place can save and enhance a slightly undecided shape.

A good decoration must be thought out beforehand in the materials that the

Plate No. 46/ Shards of different materials that have been decorated
characteristically: the translucent porcelain has
been made fragile to the utmost; the dark clays (top and bottom)
have been used in contrast to a white slip;
the grainy clay (right center) has been left unglazed
and is textured to stress its rough character.

*Plate No. 47/ A leaf is cut into the leather-hard clay.*
*The knife has been used in three different ways:*
*the main large outline has been scraped with the flat of the blade,*
*the veins of the leaf have been cut into the clay,*
*the dents on the outline of the leaf have been scratched.*
*One knife: three characteristic expressions.*

potter plans to use. It must be thought of as it will look after the transformation of the firing. (Pl. 46) The potter thus works with "abstracts," with something he can see only with his inner eye, his imagination; all the more will it be essential for him to know his materials thoroughly before he even attempts to decorate.

Also, conceive your design with your tool (Pl. 47); that means, again, not on paper, but with either a brush, a slip-tracer, a knife or whatever you choose to use. This cannot be stressed enough. Many of the lifeless designs that we see nowadays are dead because they have been translated from one medium to another without considering that much of what makes a design good is lost in this transition. The whole character or life of a line is changed if you change your tool. Watch the expression of whatever line you make and learn to see the difference between the line painted with a brush and one scratched with a dull tool, or incised with a sharp knife, or traced with slip, or pressed with a stencil. It may seem to be the same line, but what varied and characteristic expressions! (Pl. 48)

You will also have to learn to find a balance in the lines you use—an equilibrium in the lights and darks, the smooth or rough textures—for in the end the pot must remain a unity and must have no "holes." Open your eyes to the transformation in the forms caused by using either vertical or horizontal lines on a pot, or by the static or dynamic elements you choose to put on them. (Pl. 54, 55, 56, 57). Watch what happens to a foot that you make white on a dark pot, or one that you make dark on a light one; or how the proportions will seem to change if you divide your pot into linear parts, and even more, if you use different colors.

A good decoration must suit the pot when it stands in its most usual place, as on a table, not when you hold it in your hand at eye level. Being a sculptural object, the pot must be seen in the round, not as an outline but as a volume, with an inside and an outside, so that the eye can walk around its fullness; with a foot that disappears under the belly and a rim that is not only a line, but a plane, with a handle that goes out into space; the decoration must carry in its whole expression the three-dimensional space that the pot de facto holds. (Pl. 49)

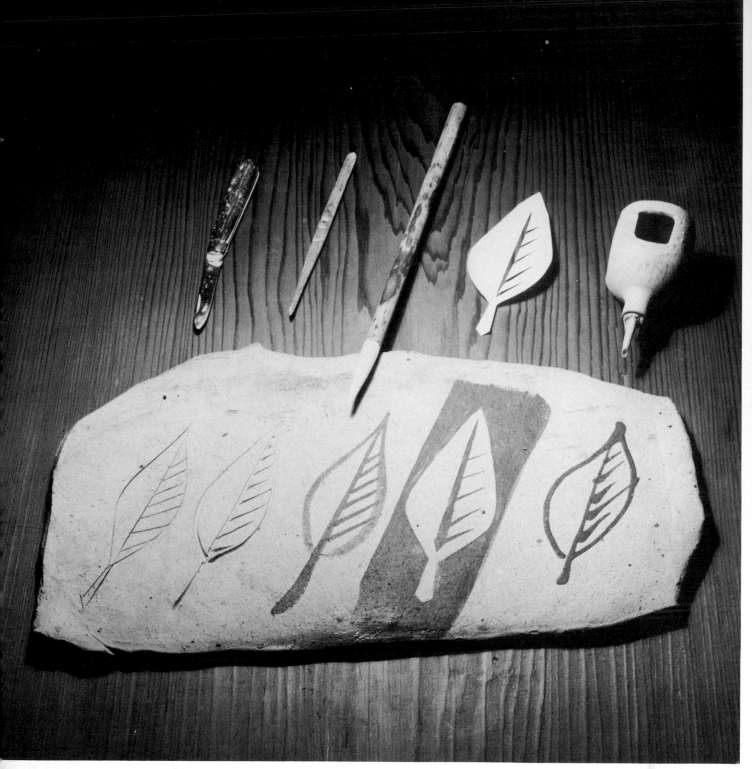

*Plate No. 48/ The same simple pattern of a leaf has been made with five different tools: a knife, a modeling tool, a paint brush, a stencil cut out of paper, a slip-tracer. Effect and expression vary with the tool.*

Don't be afraid of abstracting whatever natural form, figure of man, beast or plant you are using. You cannot start from reality; it is obvious that those forms will have to be changed, since they must do two things: fit the pot, and convey your idea of a subject. Don't take ready-made forms, but try to invent, if you can, your elements; your idea will hold them together and in place. Even if the result is awkward, it will be more honest and nearer to to real expression than an ever-so-slick imitated design. (Pl. 50)

At this point, you may have found out how instructive and inspiring it is to look deep into the forms of life around you. Plants, rocks, faces, everything that you run across and look at are part of the store of visual impressions out of which, in the end, will come the forms and ideas that you will use in your pottery. Also, you may find out that you cannot draw, that is, that your lines are dead, that they have no tension nor expression, that they do not

*Plate No. 49/ A simple black and white decoration follows the form of a simple bowl: the form and the decoration seem to be inseparable, also the clay and the glaze.*

*Plate No. 50/ An attempt at a decoration based
on T.S. Eliot's "Murder in the Cathedral." Human emotions, felt on
reading a poem, are translated into a form of pottery.*

convey what you had in mind; and it will be to your advantage to go into the study of drawing, of learning to see what is characteristic in a figure, what is accidental, what can be left out without losing the main essence, and what is all-important.

Out of my own daily experience, I know of another difficulty I should like to mention. A decoration cannot be simple enough; often, one starts with too large a concept and only reaches a fair result by eliminating one detail after another, until, in the end, only a few plain, clear lines stand.

One also has to consider the object one wants to decorate. It is obvious that there would be something ridiculous in decorating a small ashtray with, let us say, a scene from Dante's Inferno. It's not that one cannot decorate a small ashtray, or that one could not put a scene from Dante's Inferno on some fantastic pot, but those two elements are out of proportion and the combination should be avoided.

There are unlimited ways of decorating pottery. I shall mention only the most usual: slip decoration with a tracer; painting with a brush; sgraffito scratched into the soft clay; designs cut with a knife or incised with some sharp tool; patterns pressed with a stencil or inlaid in different-colored clays; painting on or under the raw or fired glaze; rolls, coils or ornaments added to the body, or sculptural patterns carved out of the pot—and all the various combinations of those methods.

On the whole, it is up to the imagination, the skill, the inventive talent of the potter. Let it be clear that there are no set rules, no preconceived patterns, or fixed techniques and formulas; there is only one actual criterion; the result must be good. The potter must explore, try, speculate, imagine, discover. Everything he has learned will help him develop his abilities, all his activities will in one way or another bring fruit to his total education, all his experiences will serve his instruction. One can learn much from others, but in the end one has to assimilate all one knows in order to find one's own materials, methods and forms; only then will the potter be able to realize his image according to his own conception and in his own way.

88

# Chapter 9 / THE GLAZE AND THE FORM

Together with its form, the most striking element of a piece of pottery is its glaze. If the form is, so to say, its bone structure, the glaze is its skin. The visual character of the glaze speaks to us very directly; in fact, for most people this is the predominant experience. It is this that either makes our mouths water and our fingers itch to touch, or makes our eyes turn away in rejection.

Such reactions are elementary and common to all people, but the more sophisticated observer will look for other qualities; he will not depend on these primitive reactions alone when judging the beauty of a glaze.

It is not of chemical components that I want to speak although they are, of course, the ingredients of the glaze and one has to be thoroughly acquainted with all of them. In one way they *are* the glaze, but they are not what will decide whether a glaze has the live beauty and the expressive character that we are aiming at. A technically perfect glaze can look horrible; in fact, many of the ugliest glazes on the commercial market are technically excellent. They do not crack, they do not bubble, craze or blister, do not run or crawl. They are perfect glazes, but ugly.

What is it then that we are looking for, and how do we fuse technical and chemical knowledge to achieve beauty? How do we unify the form of a pot (its visible sculptural element) with the character of the glaze (its visible surface)?

Each pot will, to a certain degree, require a particular type of glaze. A bright and colorful glaze might be very attractive on a small and elegant piece, to give it a jewel-like character, but the same glaze would be quite out of place on a large planter for a garden setting. Just as all dresses do not suit all

*Plate No. 51/ Pouring the glaze over a bisque pot is a skill too.*

ladies, all glazes do not suit all pots. Not only must the glaze be the right one for just that pot, it must also be the one that the potter has chosen, out of a variety of other possible ones, to convey his idea and his feeling for that special pot. The able potter can convey what he visualizes as to sculptural form during the throwing process; but he must also be competent enough to transmit what he feels through his treatment of the pot's surface and through his glaze.

Whether he achieves this through the glaze alone, or through more or less intricate and imaginative combinations of slips, textures and decors, does not matter as a principle. Whether he does it through reduction fire or salt-glazing, through over or under-firing, thick or thin glazing, or through innumerable other combinations of processes, skills and tricks, does not matter either. He has many possible ways of getting the clay, the form, and the glaze of his pot to a unity of characteristic expression. But to a single unity the pot *must* come, or it does not really come to life and is not a good pot.

It is hard for any potter to find his way through the intricate labyrinth of glaze calculations, processes, or methods of firing, and it often seems impossible to solve all the problems involved in the making of beautiful glazes. Hundreds of tests of bodies and glazes will be necessary before one gets even the slightest sense of control over all elements used. There is a way, though, that I would like to mention, a way of tackling the whole problem of glazes, after the elementary experiments have been mastered, that is less abstract and more interesting for the artist-craftsman.

As I see it, the main requirement is to avoid having a thousand different glazes, glazes taken out of books on glaze-calculation, or copied from other potters and passed on from school to school. All such glazes are impersonal, like paints bought in a store. Everybody uses them with exactly the same results. Yes, it may be that they are "fool-proof" (a favorite word in the pottery classes!) and fit every clay body. But is that all we want from a glaze? Are we not trying to say something with the glaze that is as personal and as characteristic as what we say with the form? Obviously the answer is yes, so the glaze has to be more than a well-calculated glaze formula.

*Plate No. 52/ A kiln is loaded for the first firing.*

How do we get this intimate fusion of our materials, clay, slip, glaze and fire so that our result is in accord with the primary vision we had when we started making that pot? How do we get this complete knowledge of the behavior of a glaze under every firing process and over any clay or slip we choose to apply? Definitely this whole technical know-how has to become a real creative experience to the potter before he can make *his* pot.

One can approach the problem in the following way. Let us suppose that we have one, more or less opaque, basic, white glaze that fits our clay well—this is elementary. Now let us throw a couple of dozen straight cylinders, about 5- or 6-inches high all from the same basic clay. Let us then pour every available slip—red, brown, light and dark blue, green, white, black, or whatever you have—in strips around some of those cylinders. Be sure to number everything and keep records of the results, nobody can keep it all in his head, especially in the beginning with the initial experiments. Next, let us dip the slipped cylinders into our glaze, leaving an inch or so free at the top and rubbing off another inch at the bottom. The top inch will show you what your slip looks like at firing temperature untouched by glaze, while the bottom inch will show you how very different it looks when the glaze had been poured over, but rubbed off. This will give you effects that you may want to use in contrast to glazed parts. On one single strip you will thus get three different results.

Let us go on with our experiments. Dip a few of your remaining cylinders into your glaze, covering them only half way. Then dilute your normal glaze slightly, or as you see fit, and dip the other end of the cylinders into the thinned glaze. On still other cylinders, repeat the half-and-half procedure. But this time use normal glaze and extra-thick glaze. You will discover that some glazes look better when they are applied thickly, some when they are normal, others when they are much thinned. You will also discover that each slip changes in tint, not only according to its own variation in thickness, but also according to the thickness or thinness of the glaze upon it. Thus you can have a whole series of rich color combinations with only one slip and one glaze.

With these experiments alone we would probably have more than fifty different nuances of one single glaze, but we can explore much further. Let us now treat the surface of the clay; let us make some parts really smooth or even polished, some slightly scratched, others more deeply textured. Then let us glaze these samples, again using our basic normal glaze and our thick and thin variations. Once more we will get a whole new scale of colors and effects, all different from the original ones. If we repeat these texture treatments with all our slips, there is just no end to the new, exciting combinations that develop under our hands—and all from a single glaze! As does the painter, we too have to learn to see color-values, the relationship of nuances to each other. We too have to learn to paint; just as the painter cannot merely squeeze paint from the tube, we, as potters, cannot merely glaze from the glaze-calculation-formula. Nothing alive and beautiful comes out that way.

One can go on even further. Make new cylinders out of different clay bodies, red, brown, black, and repeat the complete process using all the slips with your normal, your thinned, and your thickened glaze. You will be amazed to see how different the same slips look over a red, brown, or black clay, also how the underlying claybody will completely change the color effects of your glaze.

I need not go on. You can easily see the endless variety of nuances that you can get with a single glaze. But we still have one step further to go, the firing. We all know that the fire makes and breaks the pots, so it is most important to really know what happens in that fire, how and why your slips and glazes are affected.

Most probably your kiln will not fire the same way everywhere. The more primitive your kiln is, the more differences you will have; but this need not worry you too much if you find out *how* it fires and *where* the temperature is higher or lower than you expected. Getting acquainted with a kiln is a voyage of discovery, as exciting and surprising as a real voyage.

To find out how your kiln works, how your glazes fire at this or that spot in the kiln, you will have to place pyrometric cones and identically treated sample cylinders of your glazes at the front, back, top and bottom of your kiln. Most probably there will be an amazing range of variations and you must know all of them if you want to control the firing effects on your clay and your glaze.

Glazes also give different results in different kilns even if they are of identical construction. Each kiln has its very special way of turning out a glaze; the size of the kiln and the fuel used (gas, oil, wood, coal or electricity) as well as the speed of firing and cooling off, all matter. Even the weather or the location can interfere with and change the effect of glazes.

To a certain degree this is why pottery is so exciting to make; you are never absolutely sure how a pot is going to come out. Though you may think you know every angle of every possibility, there are always new ones; and this is good, it keeps you alert and on your toes. And I am not even talking about the genuinely different methods of firing, oxidizing or reduction, or salt-glaze firing. One needs to experience it all before one can say "this is what I wanted to make and here it is." When you have most of these fascinating elements under control you will be able to count on just about all of your pots coming out of the kiln as you expected them to. As always in pottery, it takes time and patience; whoever does not have both will never achieve excellence.

So far all the experiments that I have suggested have been made just with one glaze. But you can go on from there practically without limitation if you begin to add other materials to your glazes, or if you vary the opacity or transparency of your glazes.

It is true that anybody facing this multitude of possibilities in glaze character, surface and expression, will have a hard time deciding which ones will best convey his ideas. But as the young potter experiments, he will soon find that some glazes, slips, and textures appeal to him more than others, that they seem to give him more ideas and more new combinations for his designs. Little by little those effects that do not stimulate new feelings and thoughts will just drop out of his ceramic "vocabulary." After a while he will find his "palette," the one with which he can express whatever he wants to say. He will be able to convey his ideas in his own way because his knowledge of the glaze will not be just a chemical formula but a complete experience of the total process of making pots, an understanding of the metamorphosis of slips, glazes, and decor, knowledge of the firing process and the ability to control all these factors to suit his special purpose.

It seems to me, therefore, that much of the time and energy that is being spent in schools on glaze-calculation, trying for ever *new* glazes over and over again, could be more creatively and more stimulatingly spent on *what* to do with a glaze when you have one. Of course I am not speaking of the laboratory glaze expert in industry; I am only thinking at this point of the artist-craftsman. For us, it is not the glaze itself that gives our pot artistic value, just as it is not the tube of paint itself that gives a painter's picture its artistic value. It is what the potter does with his glaze, and what the painter does with his paint, that matters.

Anybody can copy a glaze formula from a book, or borrow one from another craftsman and get the same effect; but only accumulated knowledge from intensive study of all the ingredients used, the intimate understanding of the processes involved from the first step to the last, will give the potter superb mastery over his materials; and this can neither be imitated nor taken away from him. The continuous process of searching and finding out will, after a few years, bring to the potter a rich diversity of subtle ways of using clays and glazes, a capacity that will run parallel with his development as a human being. What he has acquired in technical knowledge in his field and in wisdom in his life, will enable him to create pots that are simple and clear expressions of his own ideas.

*Plate No. 53/ One problem: a pitcher with a rim and a belly has been given to five different students;
the results show five different expressions of one basic form.*

# Chapter 10/THE EXPRESSION AND THE FORM

We have tried to show what elements go into the making of a good pot: the hand, the material, the function, the technique, perhaps the decoration—but the total sum of all those elements only makes a functional pot that is well made, true to materials and techniques, one balanced in design, but not necessarily an expressive one, a live and warm one that conveys a personal idea and strikes a special note in the spectator's or the user's mind or heart. What element is still missing that seems to account for what is in the end the most essential part of a handmade pot?

Whether we have talked of the hands, the materials, the function, the techniques, the decoration, one word has always occurred as the touchstone of the quality: the word "expression."

Let me explain what I mean: the average basic pitcher has a belly, a neck, a foot, a spout and a handle, the relations of the parts to each other and to the whole being the sum of hundreds of years of usage and of the people's average feeling for form and beauty. In every country some special proportions and combinations of the single parts have made them look French, or Italian or Chinese. This is due to the fact that, outside of having varied needs, men also have different ideas of what is beautiful and of how they will convey these ideas in the forms of the things they make. Within the broad lines of the tribe, nation or race, there are more subtle differences as to the century or the class to which the potter belongs, and as to what sort of a man he is. Just as the true artist is able to put an experience that is common to many men into a personal and new form, so the potter who is a true potter takes an age-old form and re-forms it according to his vision, his feeling, his idea. This will not necessarily happen consciously; on the contrary, I should like to say, it will grow naturally out of the potter. At this moment, the average, basic pitcher has become a genuine, personal one and has its own unique expression. (Pl. 53) At this moment, too, that personal pot represents not only the essence of what a special man, a talented man likes, believes, feels, forms, but is representative also of the country it came from, of the whole century it was made in. For man cannot be detached from his surroundings and his time. Those very special pots in which a man's personal form-idea is fused with and becomes a crystallization of his century and his country are those that will influence his generation most, that will become the patterns for tradition until, again, other talented men in their time will transcend norm and tradition to suit a new idea and vision.

But how do these special forms develop, how do they come into the mind of a potter? How does one reach into that dreamland of forms and pictures? I can only say that the creative ability is by the grace of God—one neither deserves it nor can one expect it. But man can open himself or close himself to that grace and that is the essential point. That one can teach and learn; one can search for or reject that which is conducive to an open mind, to an imaginative response, to the developing of ideas, to a free unshackled imagination, to a wide human awareness in all things of art and of life.

From there, let us come back to our simple pitcher, the elements of which are, as we have seen, in no way rigidly fixed; they are flexible as to their relative proportions, and as to the importance of these in relation to the whole. Like the features of a human face, they are capable of unlimited variations and modulations, each of which will convey a specific expression. But, just as with some faces, some pots have a clearer, more characteristic, and distinct expression, because something in the relation of the form elements and their proportions is exceptional and more personally expressive. To discover these forms which seem to have more force to suggest an idea than have most average forms, the potter will have to make all his experiments on the basic pattern; he will have to change and modify parts and proportions (Pl. 54), add or take off as he sees fit, until, in the end, he finds a few that are characteristic and beautiful because they have a clear expression of their own. Again I say: let us not be afraid of making ugly pots; one has to make many of them to make a few good ones in the end (not all men and women are like Apollo and Venus, either). But don't let us put them all in the open market for sale and show. There are many pots that one does not

100

*Plate No. 54/ A student trying
to make a teapot explores the possibilities
by varying forms of spouts,
handles, lids, bodies.
Each pot has a different character.*

like, after a few weeks; and I think that it would be wise to keep those inside our shops or, better yet, to smash them as soon as we have been able to make better ones. But that is the main issue: we must try to make better ones, that, is, we must go on working on that basic shape that we have started from until we really get a good pot and not stop halfway from the basic and traditional one without reaching the clean new form that we are looking for.

In the treatment of the attributes (feet, handle, spout) one can be just as ingenious and experimental as in the development of the main form, also in the manipulation of the surface, in the way one varies the grain of the material or its color or texture. Two pots exactly alike as to form will look completely different if one is made of white and the other of black clay, or if you glaze the first white on the inside and dark on the outside while you do the opposite to his brother. They will not even seem to have the same proportions and certainly they will convey a quite different idea. A smooth and glossy treatment of one

*Five identical bowls have been decorated in five different ways. Plate No. 55/ 1) horizontally: it seems the broadest.*

*Plate No. 56/ 2) vertically: it seems the highest.*

pot and a roughly-incised texture on his double, a smaller or larger handle, simpler or more extravagant decorative treatment will change still more the total expression. Horizontal lines or vertical ones, the interchange of light and dark parts, the dividing into sections or the keeping of the form as a whole—all this and more lies in the hands of the potter who searches for a form that expresses specifically what he thinks is beautiful. (Pl. 55 to 59)

There is no limit to imagination: take a basic cylinder and see how many different objects can be made out of that basic shape. A cylindrical vase will most probably be the first and simplest object you will make. Then by adding a rather high foot underneath you get a beaker-vase or a chalice; with a lid a covered jar; with a spout and a handle added you can make quite a good-looking functional pitcher; or with an extra lid, a thrown spout and a handle, a coffee-pot, and so on. Each of these basic shapes can again be varied as you did

102

*Plate No. 57/ 3) diagonally: it is more dynamic.*

*Plate No. 58/ 4) the one with a texture that gives the bowl a "skin-like" expression.*

*Plate No. 59/ 5) the freely decorated one seems the smallest of all, due to the division of the main volume into parts that have been treated in various ways.*

with the pitcher above, and so you can develop a whole set of forms from each of these objects that all originated from one plain cylinder. (Pl. 60, 61, 62)

As the student works intensely and matures, his senses will develop freely and new forms that he has never seen will grow naturally and boldly from his fingers. (Pl. 63) He will give new proportions to old objects and discover new forms of his own; he will be able to secure their outlines and volumes because he is not only a creative artisan but a basically well-trained and able craftsman and worker. His pots will be alive and he will be able to make them easily and vigorously, without inhibition and restraint.

As he develops into a complete man, his pots will have something to show that is his own—something that we do not find often nowadays, a new character, a new expression.

And this is what I mean by "expression:"

As children, we all learn the letters of the alphabet, but after twenty years or more of living, working, thinking, suffering, our handwriting will have changed considerably from its first basic pattern to what is now our personal signature. Also we all learn the same words, the same language, but each of us, especially the poet, expresses with those common words that which only he can express; he takes these everyday words to fit his own vision and to convey his personal idea. Also we all have hands with five fingers and faces with eyes, a mouth and a nose; but look at the differences of expression of hands, faces, eyes and mouths according to what is, behind and beyond the average pattern of man, in the depths of each single being. This inevitable relation of the man to his piece of work will be permanently visible, the more so as he climbs to the height of his development: his pots will grow with him, in the same process, as he matures and according to the speed of his development as a man and an artist. Nothing, thus, would be more unnatural than that a man make the same pots at fifty or sixty as he made in his youth. For, if he be true to his inmost feeling, rather than to inherited tradition, success, fashion, or some literary approach, he cannot possibly want to make the same

104

*Three identical cylinders
form the bases of three different pots:
Plate No. 60/ 1) a straight vase.*

*Plate No. 61/ 2) a broad covered jar
with two handles accentuating
the horizontal movement
of lid, knob, foot and lines.*

*Plate No. 62/ 3) a tall-looking covered jar
with high foot, tall knob and lid;
the black and white decoration accentuates
the vertical expression of the whole pot.*

105

things and feel in the same way after a whole life of human experience as he did at the age of twenty-five.

So, that potter who settles down for life with one "line," whatever that may be, and wherever it came from, is not a true potter, a creative artisan; he has not matured but has become a "routineer." For routine is the accumulation of knowledge one has been taught; it is a proof of memory and skill, but not of creative intelligence and wisdom. To really know is quite something else. It is the ability to assimilate that which, one has been taught and the capacity to digest the influences of other peoples or cultures until one is able to work in his own way, according to his own ideas, in his own form-elements and techniques, and thus be capable of conceiving and inventing his own language.

Since all former techniques and forms have evolved from certain cultures at certain times as the result of deep national, racial, economic and religious reasons, it is obvious that we cannot take those forms over in their entirety, as patterns for ourselves, without their becoming false and a parody. In the realm of art, as in life, it is the spirit of man that must find the forms that are required to express the meaning of this century and its men. I realize that no one can teach another person to mature. All the more, therefore, will it be essential to eliminate obstruction and to fight errors that are apt to restrict the development of and to waste and corrupt one of man's most precious gifts, his creative imagination.

But, on the other hand, if another potter seems to be able to vary ad libitum and at any time the whole style of his work, the character of his forms, his attitude towards beauty, his techniques and apparently his ideas and his expressions with ever-so-slick technical tricks that appeal to the public--going from one extreme to the other--beware of him. The chances are that he is an over-smart business-potter and that he is only adjusting his "expression" to his sales.

Real expression is not consciously made; it grows slowly, invisibly and is.

*Plate No. 63/ A Chinese student
experiments on the basic form of a beaker vase.*

*Plate No. 64/ A Byzantine dish
of the 14th century shows the use of
elements that originated in classic Greece
nearly 2000 years before.
Victoria and Albert Museum*

108

*Plate No. 65/ The human-headed lion on this bowl probably
originated several thousand years earlier in the Sphinx of Egypt;
the form-elements from there have been assimilated into the language of a later
century and another culture. Fitzwilliam Museum, Cambridge, England*

*Plate No. 66/ This late Mycenaean krater shows
a perfect balance of form and decoration and a young vitality as
its main expression. The British Museum*

the potters used them as unconsciously as they used those of their own culture, inherited from their forefathers. (Pl. 64)

This is, for instance, a Hispano-Moresque dish decorated with a lion that has a human head (Pl. 65); most certainly this strange beast originated from the Egyptian Sphinx, but I feel pretty sure that the potter who painted that Sphinx was not conscious of using a symbol that had originated several thousand years before him in another part of the world. He just used that animal because others had used it, too, and it was an element of decoration that he was familiar with. He did not go out to copy or imitate.

Each potter made what he had to make according to the laws and limitations of his society, his own life and his talents; according to what they and he believed, according to what was needed, according to what he loved, to what he felt and thought to be beautiful. In a creative century, potters will look within themselves and their society to find inspiration and expression, from

*Plate No. 67/ Extreme sensitivity translated*
*into a philosophy of life*
*has formed this vase of the Sung dynasty.*
*The British Museum*

their own experience of life, from their contact with nature and a variety of materials, from their attitude toward man or woman, singly and in general, and above all, from their own relation to devils, gods or God. Only then does a pot become a live piece of human endeavor, something that will testify throughout the ages for the man and the culture that made it, something that has an integral quality of art such as a sculpture or a sonnet. In decadent times, on the contrary, men begin to imitate forms of cultures of other nations because their own has lost vitality and does not meet the challenge of their needs and difficulties any more; because there is no live flow of artistic understanding which the craftsman can unconsciously draw upon for his own personal need.

If we look at those six pots mentioned above, we shall see that each of our six potters has treated his material completely differently from the others, though all use basically the same clay. The late Mycenaean krater (Pl. 66) decorated with bull and bird shows a clearly conceived form, stated without

113

hesitation in a perfect tension of line and volume: handles, rim, foot are in exact balance; strong and rather unsophisticated as is the form, so also is the decoration. There was not the slightest doubt for the potter that each line had to be just where it is. To accentuate the form, the three parallel lines under the widest part of the bowl, and the one under the rim, distinctly set a certain space for the decoration which is made to fit at all cost. And if the bull with the powerful head and horns had to go down on his knees, one bending forward and the other backwards, the potter did not hesitate to make it do so, in order to solve the problem of space to his entire satisfaction. Also, if you look at the way the bird uses his legs to climb on the bull, taking advantage of one of the horns and resting on his own tail as if he were a kangaroo, you cannot help thinking that the potter greatly enjoyed painting that scene, and with gusto. His direct and imaginative treatment of space is also visible in the way he freely textured the two animals; even the eye of the bull and its tail get extra little dots here and a sort of braid there. Each line is in itself beautiful and quite tight with tension. There is only one exception: the hind leg. The lines of the back and the belly of the bull are caught up in that near horizontal-vertical black triangle of the head, before they escape again, together and parallel, in the horns, accompanied by the lesser accord of the two legs of the bird. All this is in perfect harmony and gives a vibrating sonority that is, I feel, truly Mediterranean.

In contrast, let us view the Chinese Temmoku vase (Pl. 67) of the Sung dynasty. How elegant, how delicately subtle is that form with the specially narrow neck and the opening of the rim like a flower! But how old too, how world-wise, disillusioned, tired and slightly decadent (compared with the young vitality of the Mycenaean krater) is the soft line of the slightly hanging belly: it is just a trifle too heavy, too lazy to stand up of its own tension and it seems to want to compensate for the ethereal longing of the over-sensitive neck. The glaze and the decoration, too, reflect sophistication; and the elusive surface treatment would never have occurred to the mind and senses of the much simpler Greek; like an Oriental smile that is half sorrow and half joy, it conveys a background of centuries of human experience, it is full of doubts, of questions half-answered, of half and quarter tones, of unclear and semi-clear forms that are not meant purely as forms but as the essence of a philosophy of life that expresses itself here. It is no longer a thing, an

114

*Plate No. 72/ These prehistoric bowls show that simple forms and plain decorations make good pots. Victoria and Albert Museum*

Plate No. 73/ A medieval English jug
has been simply tooled
on the spinning wheel. Circular
lines texture the sensitive
but strong outline of this jug.
The British Museum

Plate No. 74/ An English 14th century
tile shows a pattern inlaid
with light clay in a darker matrix clay.
Victoria and Albert Museum

Greek krater, nor of the beauty of the Sung vase. But it has something that is very near to us, that we all know, something that many a potter in the old countries can still make for his girl, something that is much more conventional and naturalistic than the other two pots and that represents an attitude our generation is just beginning to escape from: it is unmistakably bourgeois. In its forms it is still good; proportions are clearly seen though there is a slightly loose extravagance and laissez-aller in the whole thing: the handles are a bit over-relaxed, especially the right one (as a potter, I can see that he made the left one first and had difficulties in making the second one exactly the same shape), the wide foot and the narrow base under the bowl act as a good pedestal to the goblet and to the figure. The division of the volumes definitely shows a classic background that has, if we want to put it that way, degenerated or re-developed into a personal 16th century expression. I think there is no doubt that the figurehead is a rather naturalistic portrait and not an imaginary lady, and surely the art historian could tell by the clothing and the hairdo from what class this lady comes.

Our fourth pot, a Chimu jug from Peru (Pl. 69), suggests for us a completely different state of mind. First and foremost, our immediate reaction is: "This is a sculpture." This is not just a clear symmetrical form thrown on the wheel, but a complex of different parts modeled together; some parts are added, others carved out of the body. The whole subject is treated like architecture which carries certain main bodies of great weight, and these, in turn, carry the smaller volumes.

The fine sense of values of masses in relation to each other, and to the whole, is characteristic of the Chimu pots: one cannot help admiring the sureness of the feeling of the potter who cut that head so clearly and so strongly, while that hand on the belly was flattened out to so slight a thickness as to keep the whole flask round. It was essential not to obstruct with too strong detail the mighty impression the head was supposed to give. How lovely also is that decoration at the front of the belly, not added, but carved out this time, forming a third plane in the high parts of the lines and dots and a fourth plane in the deeper parts that have been carved out. And all of this occurs within the one thickness of the pot. The jug also has two fronts, one on each side of the two main bodies, that force the spectator and the user to see it in the round;

120

Plate No. 75a/ Greek Mastos, black figure
on light background. A perfect balance
of live form and expressive
decoration. (from Paul Jacobsthal:
Ornamente Griechischer Vasen, Berlin 1927)
The British Museum

Plate No. 75/ A pattern scratched through
the white slip shows the
underlying darker clay body of this
huge jar from Iquitos, The Amazon, Peru.
The British Museum

*Plate No. 76/ Three bowls from the Nazca culture (Peru) show imaginative treatment of the same basic form and of the same decorative element. Musée de l'Homme, Paris*

there is no front because there is no real back and the interest will continuously move around the pot—this is a very sculptural attitude. The material is plain grey-black clay—no painting, no glaze, just free form. But in spite of the restraint in the use of the material and the sculptural discipline the Chimu potter has shown, there is a magic essence apparent that radiates from the whole structure and that one cannot escape. I do not think that this was accidental, but rather well within the conscious problem that the Chimu potter had to solve.

Our next example of pottery is a Persian dish of the 13th century with a lion painted in blue and black against a background of plants. (Pl. 70) The form of this dish, as form, is practically non-existent—I mean, the dish is only the background for a beautiful decoration, and is not in itself of any importance, nor has it any definite expression and shape. The only important thing is the painting on it, and that is indeed of first quality. The swiftness of the lines, the excellent drawing of the beast and all its details—feet, eye, eyelashes and hair, mouth and nostrils—show that this plate was drawn by an expert craftsman, an elegant draftsman, a painter rather than a potter. The whole decoration has something of a weaving, an interlacing of form-elements against a background that is painted like a tapestry. This is meant to fill out any empty space between the legs, under the head and behind the back. Nowhere

122

*Plate No. 77/ A freely scratched ornament decorates this aryballos-type urn from Peru.
Musée de l'Homme, Paris*

is the bare clay to be seen: it is all lush glaze, line, spots, dots, arabesques. Even where the painter has meant to show a light animal against the darker background, he could not bear to leave it just as the light glaze would have made it. No, he dotted and even speckled it all over with tiny speckles, three at a time in small triangles, so as to have an allover pattern, something that covered the dish from edge to edge and almost burst its limits. Both the head and the tail of our animal had to be squeezed into the rim of the dish, showing distinctly that the painter was not so much interested in the form as in the painting. If you look back at the Greek krater with the bull, you will see why I called the decorator of the Persian dish a painter and not a potter. The colors, the light effects on the lush glaze, the richness of design and variety of form-elements in it give to the bowl a splendor and a sensuous intensity that is very expressive and quite unique.

*Plate No. 78/ This large jar from Susa is
an excellent example of how a plain
pot made throughout the centuries for daily
use can be an expressive and exciting
piece of pottery if the potter
is talented and remains alert and
open to his material and its possibilities.*

*Plate No. 79/ The crackle glaze and the fluidity of the decoration*
*give a glassy appearance to this vase from Persia, 13th century.*
*The clay has disappeared as a decorative element. Victoria and Albert Museum*

*Plate No. 80/ A Persian dish from Aleppo, 13th century.*
*The decoration covers the dish from*
*edge to edge and has become all-important.*
*The effects of melting the glaze*
*in the fire are used freely without*
*too much concern for the form. The British Museum*

126

And now we shall look at a pot of our own generation and our own culture: a pot of Frans Wildenhain's. (Pl. 71) Here, for the first time again after centuries of experimenting with glaze effects, we find a potter who consciously renounces that surface glamour and goes back to the old relation of clay to form. Just as his ancestors did thousands of years ago, he uses the clay only and gives it form and life.

The clearness and simplicity of the grey unglazed material and the excellent relation of the parts to the main body give exactness to the form and accentuate the sculptural quality of the whole urn. The handles show a tightness, a dynamic tension and a certain abstractness in the way they jut out at right angles from the urn, swell up to their highest point and taper off to a precise angle at their junction with the main body. The knob too is characteristic: it rises from the nearly horizontal lid in a powerfully exact curve, so that the whole pot ends on a sober, unsentimental horizontal plane.

There is no doubt about it: this pot was made in our times; it is no copy, no relic from former cultures, no imitation of techniques that were developed by other men, other races or former centuries. Only the basic techniques of all potters have been used, the throwing on the wheel, and the old material, clay, ——but they have been used by an imaginative and creative man, they have developed into a pot of our time. A well-defined and clear-cut idea of a modern man has transcended the age-old craft with a new vitality: the pot again has that magic quality we found in the old Chimu pot from Peru. There is no doubt as to the masterly competence, the awareness, the vigor and the honesty of the man who made this pot; he hides nothing and adds nothing that is not essential and expressive. The result is an excellent modern pot.

With these six examples, I have wanted merely to give an idea of a few of the possibilities of expression and of treatment that lie in our material, basically so formless. Still, in spite of all the differences in pottery one can divide the whole large family of potters into just two main camps: the cultures that have used clay alone without any glaze at all, and those that have invented, made and perfected glazed pottery.

*Plate No. 81/ A Chinese incense burner of the Yuan dynasty (1280-1368)
shows a powerful form with a sensitive impressionistic brush decoration.
Victoria and Albert Museum*

128

All primitive men have used clay only; they have used all sorts of ingenious devices to vary the looks, the character, the expression of that basic material. They have incised patterns (Pl.72), they have used stencils, they have pressed tools into the clay (Pl. 73), they have inlaid lighter clays in a darker matrix clay (Pl. 74), they have covered a dark body with a lighter slip and have scratched out patterns, they have painted with red, white and black clays, designs and ornaments (Pl. 75, 76); they have also carved decorations out of the surface of the pot or added, modeled or pressed designs (Pl. 42), geometrical ornaments, figures or animals, dots, coils and other free forms (Pl. 69, 77).

For all those cultures that used no glaze, it is obvious that the pots had to stand by their sculptural quality mainly, that is, by the clearness and excellency of their shape. The form was thus all-important and had to be significant

*Plate No. 82/ White bowl from Persia, pierced and incised with a delicate decoration. The incurved blue rim gives force to a delicate surface treatment. Fitzwilliam Museum*

*Plate No. 83/ An elaborate Hispano-Moresque dish has
an eagle incised and painted over its entire surface. The dish itself,
so to say, no longer exists as a sculptural form. Fitzwilliam Museum*

in the use for which it was meant. (Pl. 78) In the best times of those cultures, the pot remained a sculptural, three-dimensional object, and the decoration was secondary to the form. I mean that it was conceived in such a way as to fit and to accentuate the form and not to hide nor exceed it; it was an additional element with which the potter stressed in another medium what he had tried to convey with his forms. I am, of course, not talking about the subjects of the decoration, why they were such and what they represent; these are very interesting to study, too, but they are the problem of the art historian and anthropologist. As a potter, I only look at the creative problems that faced one of the potters of former times and what he did to solve them. Those ancient potters used decoration very consciously and with powerful directness without concern for the naturalness or correctness of the forms that they took over from nature. Since it was more the line that counted than the color, they

130

developed an extraordinary facility for drawing; they abstracted, without fear, the size, movements, expressions of the beings that they painted on their pots to suit the form they were decorating. (Pl. 66) We moderns can and have learned much from them. They developed symbols that were like shorthand signs for things that they believed in or adored, that they could scratch or paint on a pot and that would convey to their fellow men the ideas they had, easily without words and with a minimum of form-elements. (Pl. 76, 78) Thus, in spite of using only clay, they seem to have found an extraordinary range of different treatments and varied into many expressions the one basic material. They must have believed in some special power or a God-given or God-willed quality in that material, something that was as inexhaustible and as incomprehensible and baffling as life itself. We find in Pliny a remark to this effect that has struck me as well worth recording: "Even at the present day in the midst of such wealth as we possess, we make our first libation at a sacrifice not from vessels of precious stone or crystal, but from ladles made of earthenware, and that in the ineffable bounty of the earth———."

The second camp of our family of potters, the one that developed and mainly made glazed pots, changed the whole outlook of man on pottery. With the discovery of glass and glaze, with the use of color, not as a slip but as a melting agent and a glass (Pl. 79), that is, with an optical effect of light that was either radiated or absorbed through the glaze, a whole new set of expressions became possible.

The pot became more and more something to paint on, something that was only complete when it was covered with a colored glaze, or decorated, if it had a plain one. (Pl. 80) The surface became the prominent part of the pot, something that in itself had a right to be, that could be metamorphosed in an unending variety of small, delicate, impressionistic treatments, something that allowed for the slightest emotional and intellectual distinctions (Pl. 81), something as ephemeral and evanescent as the light on the clouds or the rainbow. The form disappeared in proportion as the surface grew in importance.

The techniques invented were as manifold as the effects required: turquoise, tin and lustre glazes came from the Middle East and flooded Italy, Spain, France and all of Western Europe. The faience industry then developed, first

134

*Plate No. 87/ Freedom of design can be simple and unsophisticated as in this bowl from Persia or Mesopotamia (8th to 10th century). Victoria and Albert Museum*

*Plate No. 88/ A Chinese flask of the Tang dynasty shows sculptural sensitivity, restraint and strength. Victoria and Albert Museum*

136

in Faenza and Majorca, later all over France, Belgium, Holland and Germany. Salt-glazed stoneware was made throughout the centuries in Germany and England; celadon and other glazes from China came to Europe, too, and enriched time and again the surfaces of pots. It was like a new burst of power; there was no end to what was tried out and invented. (Pl. 82, 83, 84, 85, 86, 87) Potters were discovering a freedom of expression (self-expression) that they had never been able even to imagine before; it was something akin to the way of our modern French artists who are discovering pottery as a medium to express certain things that they had never thought of before. (Picasso, Lurcat)

But in all those fantastic, sometimes unimaginably lovely pots, we rarely see one in which the main thing is apparent, I mean the clay. Of course it influences to a great extent the whole look of the pot, through the transformation that the clays give to the glaze. But the pots do not stand any more in the grand natural bareness of their earthy material, an intrinsic part of nature herself, like rocks, with textures, lines and spots of color here and there; they are now always dressed up, magnificently dressed up, if you like, but still, I should like to say, they are not more beautiful than when they stood in their original naked grandeur. (Pl. 66, 69, 77 & 78)

*Plate No. 89/*
*Kanjiro Kawai uses old techniques*
*in a structural way.*
*(Japan, 20th century)*

137

*Plate No. 90/ A planter has evolved a new form under the hands of Robert Turner.*
*(USA, 20th century) The form, the material and the glaze are fused in one expression.*

Since life has a way of swinging us, as with the pendulum, from one end to the other, we find in our times that we are now a trifle tired of all those gorgeous colors, of all those decorations. We no longer believe in the values of those too sensuous surfaces, those impressionistic glazes that look like rainbows and cloudy skies, fiery outbursts of volcanoes, desert sunsets or Pacific blues. We are slowly looking for more subdued tones, for a simpler and nearer relation to our original material again. Now that man has learned what he can do with his ceramic techniques, he begins to be selective as to what these convey to him in the expression of his whole life. (Pl. 92) It is natural and good that our pots should reflect our ideas, and so we see a tendency towards a more structural form (Pl. 91) and a more dynamic expression (Pl. 71) of the whole pot, displacing the up-to-now all-important treatment of the surface only. The modern potters will thus show pots with textures cut out directly in the clay (Pl. 56, 57, 58, 59, 89 & 92), with glazes of a more subdued color range (Pl. 50,94); also pots without glaze (Pl. 71), or only partly glazed––even pots that are not round any more nor symmetrical but free in form. (Pl. 90)

The modern potter is trying again to find on his own some ways of forming, in a timeworn and often much abused material, those ideas that occupy him today. (Pl. 91)

138

*Plate No. 91/ Covered jar:*
*A personal expression of an age-old object.*
*M. Wildenhain (USA, 20th century)*

*Plate No. 92/ The potter of today cannot escape from the problems of his time: abstraction is in his thoughts and there is no limit to the form-elements that he invents. A rectangular container by Dirk Hubers (Holland, 20th century)*

The inventions, tools and procedures, the newly discovered materials, methods and machines have forced him out of a comfortable and complacent sleep in tradition and convention. The values of a hundred years ago are not his any more and he has found out that he has to go back to a more basic, sounder treatment of his pottery, to something that is nearer the original and primitive approach of man to clay. (Pl. 95) We can only welcome this; it is an exciting and hopeful, though difficult situation for the potters, but the effort needed makes us grow——and that is the essential.

For man created pots after his own image, from a clay that he dug somewhere near the place where he was living. He made his pots to suit his needs, all of them, corporeal, religious, ethical, esthetical. He made his pots to use daily, to live with, and sometimes to be buried in.

140

*Plate No. 93/ A deeply-textured glaze has an expression of its own.*
*A bowl by Gertrud and Otto Natzler (USA, 20th century)*

In all ages there have been potters, some talented, and some not-so-talented; at all times there have been good, expressive pots and live ones and also insensitive, unimaginative and dull ones. The past has an advantage over the present: the pots that we see from former centuries in museums or collections have been chosen for their special value and beauty and are not characteristic of the whole production of a century. We may be tempted thus to think that the older potters were much more talented than ours. I do not know if that could be proved. I believe rather that some eras have been more propitious to crafts than ours, so that they have carried the struggling craftsman more easily than in modern times. Also, there were times when the crafts were the basic occupation of a great part of the population, from which the more talented artisan could rise uninhibited and with full-fledged knowledge of his profession, a fact that does not exist any more and that we badly miss. Today, the effort of creation must be carried by the craftsman singly and often in opposition to the society in which he is living. This requires a much stronger personality and a greater amount of talent than in those times when the whole of society carried the craftsman.

141

Thus, today we mostly know the artist by his name, formerly perhaps by the workshop he worked in. I do not think that one must deduce from this that our potters have no humility or that the moderns are arrogant. Since there are no workshops to carry the single man, each of us is forced to stand on his own feet and is naturally known by his own name. Many exceptional potters from antiquity are well known by their names, too; in fact they have often written them in clear letters right around their pots without inhibition: Epictetus, Duris, Kachrylion and others. And why not? Man has a right to honest pride in his work, and it takes courage to sign your name for eternity on a piece from your own hand, not wanting to escape the judgment of future generations. But for the many pots that were signed there were millions of anonymous ones, many of which were excellent too. To distinguish the better ones among the un-limited number of pots that man has made, and, from the better ones, the very best, should be a potter's aim and job. That this is not easy is evident. Just as nature creates innumerable plants that all have specific and characteristic forms according to what they are meant to be, and life as a whole is made of an unending variety and complexity of elements, so it is also with man's most basic occupation. It is the nearly limitless variations and modulations on the theme "pot" that make "Pottery." If we look around us with open eyes we will see that there is no one solution for pottery, just as there is no one color of race, nor one variety of animal or plant; neither is there one way of making pottery that is better in itself than another, the methods and techniques are all equal under the sun. It is what we are able to do with them that matters.

We may tend to admire the pottery of some country or of a given period for a certain character in it that appeals to us or is akin to what we think and feel; or we may find the work of another not to our liking or alien to our conception. But let us beware of putting them into first or second classes or in higher or lower orders of beauty.

It would be difficult to imagine an Incan chief (if it were possible in time) liking a classic French vase of the eighteenth century, or, the other way around, a French lady of that period not being thoroughly shocked at the "ugliness" of an Incan pot. And yet, both pots have their intrinsic beauties, that we, later comers, can easily see today; and so we are able to appreciate the one and the other.

*Plate No. 94/ A textured surface can fit the bowl like a skin. M. Wildenhain (USA, 20th century)*

Thus, let us look at the pots that men have made before our time, and are still making in our days with open eyes, with free, observing senses and mind, without preconceived ideas of what is "beautiful;" let us admire and learn from all the good pots that man has made, let us try to discern what makes some of them (not so very many!) so alive, good, eternally fresh, expressive and true. Let us be moved by them, for this emotion will be fertile and generous for the growing potter, it will open his mind and widen his heart, it will keep him free from petty jealousy. He will recognize the really good pots by the way his heart throbs with something akin to the emotion of love when he encounters one. He will learn to see that truly the pot is the image of the man and he will understand the latter through the former.

For, whether ancient or modern, Chinese, French, American or Incan, throughout all the world and at all times, the common denominator of all pottery is man.

# Chapter 12 / AN IMAGINARY DIALOGUE BETWEEN A STUDENT AND A POTTER

Student:  How long will it take me to learn to make pottery?

Potter:    It all depends on what you call "Pottery."

St:    I mean when shall I be able to throw pots and glaze them and fire them well enough to show and sell?

Po:    You surely realize that to show and sell is in no way a criterion of the quality of a pot.  It only depends on who the jury of a show is, or who buys the pots; depending on the taste and knowledge of those people, the good or bad pots are exhibited, prized and sold.

St:    Well, then, how long did it take you to make good pots, if I may ask?

Po:    It seems to me that I'm still learning to make them, though I've been at it for some thirty-odd years.  I still feel that only very rarely does a good piece come out of my hands.  Why does that shock you?

St:    I think that you are perhaps too critical.

Po:    One can't be too critical.  That's what makes you grow, the feeling that whatever you have made could have been much better.  And then you try to make it so next time.

St:    Then let me put my question this way: when shall I be able to teach, or when can I make a living out of it?

Po:    Why do you want to teach and what makes you think you have a right to teach?  You surely must realize it takes a very sound and thorough knowledge of potting to be able to teach it——much more than most beginners have when they come out of college.  You must have certain abilities, too, and you'll have to look the whole field over in its total width before you'll be able to choose what is essential to teach a student. As T. H. Huxley once put it: "The power of teaching a little depends on knowing a great deal, and that thoroughly." After some years of work and experience, you might become quite a good teacher, but first, if I were you, I'd go out into the world and try to make pots myself before I'd try to teach others how to make them.

St: But I have to make a living, and apparently it's almost impossible to make a living at potting.

Po: We should first define what you call "a living," and also find out why you want to make pottery.

St: I want to make pottery because I got interested in it at college; and since there is a widespread interest in pottery now, there'll be a need for teachers.

Po: Isn't that a rather materialistic point of view? If we should need opera singers tomorrow, you'd learn to sing. Am I right? Doesn't it seem rather strange for you to want to learn something, which requires very special aptitudes, just because some people are going to need teachers? How could you go in for singing without having a voice? Don't you know that potters must have certain talents, too? Just as a singer must have a voice, a potter must have a feeling for form.

St: Can't anyone learn to make pottery? If he learns the techniques, anybody should be able to make pots.

Po: That's what many people think; all you have to do is look around and perhaps you'll change your mind! If you start thinking about what it takes to learn a craft, you'll realize that not everyone is made for that sort of life.

St: Well, what is a craft? Isn't it just a profession like any other?

Po: No, a craft is an occupation that requires skill, strength, cunning; all this

146

lies in the Anglo-Saxon word "craeft;" not just a profession, but a profession that needs more than mere labor. It takes a human being who has learned and acquired a skill, who is strong in his individuality: cunning, resourceful, and inventive, unconventional and free.  And all this is not in relation to outward success, as many are, but in relation to a man's work, as few are.  Now, in our days, there are many who make pottery but, as you have just said, few make a living out of it.  Do you know why?

St:  Because the public isn't really interested in pottery as an art and there's too much competition from cheaper factory work, the things made by machine.

Po:  I don't think that's the only reason, though potters flatter themselves with that excuse.  I think the difficulty lies with the potters, too, and not only with the public in general.  Don't forget, all of us——you and I——are the public, too.  Maybe there was something in the way those craftsmen of old worked and lived that accounted for just that difference.  What was different between them and us is that, in spite of all our techniques and progress, they were apparently ahead of us in skill and the living craft.

Let me explain this by showing that it's our way of life and their way of life that seem to account for most of the difference.  The ancient potter from Greece or from France or China or Italy was a potter, nothing more—— but, also, nothing less.  He began learning his craft when he was a boy, generally from his father who, again, had learned it from his father.  He knew all about the difficulties, the joys, the struggles of pottery long before he began learning it.  He heard talk about pottery from the time he could understand the meaning of words.  He used pottery every day drinking and eating from it, or bringing libations to the ancient gods.  For him, pottery was not a luxury nor some miserable little bowl used now and then.  No, it was something so closely related to his life that he was never detached from it: when you were born, you were washed in a big bowl; when you died, some precious piece of pottery went with you into the great unknown.  It was a part of the most trivial occupation and of the most highly religious acts: in a word, it was "alive."

147

St: This is all true, but let's not be sentimental: we cannot live as they did. Times have changed. Our tempo is much faster and, somehow, every one of us has to adjust himself to the society he lives in——at least to a certain degree.

Po: Why? And who says we should adjust ourselves to society, instead of adjusting society? I'll come back to that in a minute, when we talk about making a living. Right now, let's follow the way a boy long ago went into his craft and see whether we can't learn something.

That boy, this future master-craftsman, perhaps, went into an apprenticeship to a good master. It was a hard school of learning, day by day, on the potter's wheel. No difficulties were solved for him; he had to work his way out——learn, struggle, despair and learn again. There were thousands of pitfalls, temptations to do things easily, carelessly, badly. But because the standards of work, and of honest labor, because a man's pride in his craft were high, there was no place for mediocre workmanship and for work half-done, or for semi-devotion to the job. For those craftsmen knew well that the god of the potter is like Jehovah of the Old Testament: that you had to believe in him wholly, with all your strength, with all your might and with all your will.

So, when the boy came through his apprenticeship, he knew his craft: that is, he knew how to make a jug, a plate, a bowl and all the rest of the pottery that was in daily use. He also had a certain idea of how a craftsman was supposed to live and work: that was part of his apprenticeship. Still, he was a long way from being a master. Do you know why?

St: Do you mean because he hadn't been on his own and proved he could make pottery without the help of a master?

Po: No, not quite. That isn't exactly the difference between what they called a journeyman and a master. The potter we are talking about could make any pot at any time he was ordered to; but he wasn't yet a man who had developed his own ideas of pots, a man who had invented new techniques and new forms, who had said something with his pottery that no one had ever said quite that way before.

148

Plate No. 96/ *A potter talks to some students: to learn to think,
to work, to develop as a craftsman is a lifetime job, and it is worthwhile.*

This, he could not learn from someone else; this, no master could teach him. He alone was responsible for whether he would develop from a journeyman into a master. He knew that to make pottery well and as it should be––alive, imaginative, formful, healthy in its relation to life–– was a full man's job. That, those old potters never doubted. They gave their full energies: conscientiousness, work-discipline––all those good qualities that every truly valuable work requires. And they also gave their talent, their imagination and their faith. They never questioned that the whole thing was worth the effort.

St: I can see now that you can't know whether you're made for that sort of life and work; whether you have the guts and the patience and the talent, when you are just starting to learn. I see what you mean; you'd have to make pottery to find out. But then, how could I live during that time?

Po: Exactly, and here we are, back at our first argument about the matter of making "a living." Just what do you mean by "a living?" Can you tell me quickly what you need to be able to live?

St: Well, there is, of course, food and lodging that we all need.

Po: To earn this shouldn't be too difficult, even today. With your education in ceramics, you certainly should be able to earn that much, even if you had no talent at all. You know how to make certain things, you can throw––

St: No, not very well yet. I've had too little practice––barely a few hours a week.

Po: Well, then, go and learn it. How could you teach if you don't even know the fundamentals? First of all, go to some good potter and work for him half days and work for yourself the other half day; you know about glazes and firing techniques, you can make plaster molds and what not. It shouldn't be impossible for you to get a job in a factory; that's very instructive, too, and you can learn a lot there from the other workers. You can always learn from other people; and potters, more than anyone else, should have their eyes wide open.

150

St: Yes, but there are still other things you need———

Po: Oh, I know: nice clothes, a car, a telephone, a refrigerator, a washing machine, a radio and even, if possible, a television set. Is that what you mean?

St: Yes. There are so many things that are necessary; and if you can't earn enough to buy them, you feel frustrated and unhappy. You can't compete with the other fellow.

Po: But who says you're not going to be able to? Why don't you take a chance on making a living? Why would you rather drop your main interest and go in for a career of teaching (for which you may not be really suited), instead of making a try at pottery? Suppose you had a car––you have, I see––well, don't you take chances every day of being killed or maimed for life without giving it a thought?––just because you want to get around fast? Isn't that taking much more of a chance for much less? Don't you think that the pottery you profess to be interested in, which you have been studying for three or four years in college––don't you think pottery is well worth trying––to see if you can make a go of it? Isn't it a much smaller risk than taking your life in your hands driving a car?

St: Yes, but what about setting up a shop? That costs a lot of money. How can a beginner possibly pay for it?

Po: I think you're exaggerating the cost; it needn't be exorbitant; you can make a lot of decent pots with simple equipment: a kiln, a couple of kick wheels, some laundry trays and some bins for clay, some shelving and planks––and that's about all you'd need to start with. Of course, materials are not always cheap, but the expensive ones are not necessarily the best. Potters have to learn to make much out of little. (Pl. 95) That's a basic bit of wisdom in the potter's craft––and, for all I know, in life, too: to learn much, to need little.

St: But don't you think you've got to have some machinery too: a pug mill, a ball mill, an electric wheel?

Po: If you have the money to buy them, certainly it will help; but if you haven't, don't think you can't make pots without them. Especially the electric wheel. It's fine when you know how to throw and are going in for production——but I always advise any student to work on a plain kick wheel; there is a much closer connection between the potter and the pot, an intimate relation akin to a dance between the different parts of the body of the potter and his work——a relation that one cannot have with the electric wheel. You may laugh if I tell you that I'm still working with the simple equipment that I listed just now, and that I have probably made more than twenty thousand pots with them. I don't say that I don't sometimes wish I had a small pug mill and other machinery to help me, but you have to pay for everything you buy and these machines have not yet been worth the money to me. Besides, all you American men are so ingenious and mechanically-minded it would surely be quite easy for you to devise some contraption to help with most of the mechanical work. Surely you won't starve——few people die of starvation in our lucky country.

St: Oh, I'm not really afraid of starving, but I'm afraid that it might take me years——or my whole life to earn a decent living.

Po: And even if it did, or if it really were a bit hard in the first years, or throughout your whole life, don't forget how you would grow in the experience of making your own way with integrity and according to your innermost wishes, and without having to conform to an alien schedule or rhythm and without having to take money (I mean a salary) from a school or from students, for something that you aren't really equipped to teach as well as you should be. Don't you feel that this teaching proposition is not quite a clean and honest situation for you?

St: I've never thought of it that way; so many others do it, why shouldn't I?

Po: We're talking about you. Let's leave the others out of the picture. As I see you, you are apparently not willing, or you're afraid of giving your all to that great venture: Pottery. Where, in our hurried times, shall we find men and women who have the training and the patience, the skill and

152

the faith in the value of their work, and of a life dedicated to it that the old craftsmen had? We find all those qualities in the scientific field. Why not in the arts and crafts? Why must we always go fast: a few weeks, a term perhaps, and teachers' jobs are offered to those who haven't even proved they are qualified for a hopeful apprenticeship. How can anything but the crudest sort of makeshift handwork come out out of it? No wonder those people can't make a living.

St: But as a teacher, one can make a living and make pots too. Isn't that an ideal setup?

Po: To teach and to make pots does seem an ideal setup; but in practice the teacher usually is so preoccupied with teaching that he has little time left to pot——or, if he pots, he won't be able to do much teaching. Each occupation really requires all a man has to give. And as to those "others" you were referring to just now, they may have had completely different reasons for going into teaching. No two situations are alike; no two men are the same. What may have been right for them because it was according to their capacities need not necessarily be right for you. And then again, there are some "born teachers," but they are as rare as born potters. Also, it's quite possible that some make better teachers than they would have been free potters. Others, again, may be perfect for small-scale industry——or perhaps even large-scale industry——because that's their capacity. Of course they'll make more money than you do, and if that is what you're mainly looking for, I say go to it.

St: What bothers me most is that as a teacher or as an industrialist, you are considered a good, and important member of society. But as an "artist," you're looked on almost with contempt, or as if you were not quite normal. Actually, you seem to stand outside of the community.

Po: I have not found it so. But if you play up the "artist," that could happen to you——but why do it? You are a potter, that's all. Leave it to your descendants to decide whether or not you were an artist. Besides, there are other communities in the world, broader than the ones you are talking about, where all real men and women talk the same language, no matter what tongue they use. To such a community you will belong if, instead of doing blindly what everyone does, you do what you think is right, straight and honestly and as well as you can. There's no disgrace in having your own picture of what life and the world should be. We need men and women who are ready to form their lives according to their work, who are determined to study and to learn before they start teaching and showing and selling: individuals who are honest enough to recognize their own limitations and have enough integrity to be craftsmen (and I mean craftsmen at their best, not dilettantes). This requires more than the mere knowledge of techniques. It takes the whole of human experience, a relationship to nature, to the animals, to your fellow man, and to those things that cannot be put into words. It takes in all the background of the centuries that have molded us and our way of thinking and feeling.

Also, when you talk about "a living," don't you think that the freedom you'll enjoy, if you're doing what you believe in, if you're doing it on your own time and according to your personal conscience and judgment––don't you think this freedom, this standing on your own feet, with work made by your own hands, without having to kowtow to anybody; this great and beautiful freedom of doing what you like best, the best way you can–– don't you think it's worth while taking a few years of tough work in stride for that? To me, it's depressing to see that, in America, which was founded on those very ideas, our youth has not the courage and the idealism the pioneers had. Doesn't it seem a shame to you, too?

St:  Perhaps; but of course you can't deny there is no security in that way of life.

Po:  Do you know what Shakespeare says in Macbeth about security? "Security is mortals' chiefest enemy." Let us have the courage to risk our so-called security (which does not exist anyway), for an idea that is the essence of what man was made for, namely, to be free, in a life dedicated to work that has dignity, a work that he loves and does well. You can be sure, too, that it's true––God helps you if you help yourself. But why should anyone help someone else who isn't willing himself to make a real effort? The real battles of life are fought within our hearts––that's where defeat or victory begins.

154

*Plate No. 97/ The tools of a potter who works on the wheel: the simpler the better.*
*A knife, a rib, outside tool, inside tool, a wire, a sponge, a small modeling tool and a signet.*

St: Sometimes I wonder whether it makes any sense at all to learn doing things by hand today, when the machine can easily produce all we need; and whether it wouldn't be better to go in for industrial design instead of making pots by hand.

Po: Yes, that is an all-important issue. Personally, I think that it will always make sense for some men and women to make things by hand in their own free way, on their own free time, according to their own conceptions. But it is a fact that there is no need in our day for the reproducing craftsman, the man who made the same pot a thousand times, who from his youth to his death was only a repeating worker. Today, we do that work with the machine and I think that it would be unreasonable for any craftsman to try to solve a production problem by hand. No, let the machine do that, and free the craftsman to be an inventor and explorer in his field. The difficulty is, of course, that only a limited few will be able to make the grade; I mean, be capable of always growing with and in their work.

As to industrial design, I certainly think that the craftsman should think in terms of it, too and look for cooperation with industry, but certainly not until he has mastered his craft thoroughly, and has absorbed, and understood most of the difficulties of materials, techniques, processes, and the basic problems of form. I also think that small productive workshops which rely more for their success on quality than on quantity may be a good solution for many a young potter. Not all of us are capable of being creative artisans; and it is a matter of honestly finding out your limitations and your capacities and then going in for what is best suited to you. For, in the end, you know, it will depend on how you feel and think about life and what you were made for.

To make a living doesn't mean merely being able to eat and drink––man does not live by bread alone. "For what shall it profit a man, if he shall gain the whole world, and lose his own soul?" (Mark 8:36) Consider that.

St: It seems to me that we're talking about philosophy rather than about pottery.

156

*Designed by Sydney Butchkes*